PRAYERS OF VIA DE CRISTO

PRAYERS OF VIA DE CRISTO

CALLS TO WORSHIP
FOR
PROGRESSIVE
CHRISTIANS

JAMES BURROUGHS ARMSTRONG

ISBN-13: 978-0692457931 (JimBooks)

ACKNOWLEDGEMENTS

Via de Cristo United Methodist Fellowship is a remarkable Progressive Christian fellowship, planted and nurtured in its earliest formative years by Reverend David Felton, and more recently pastored by Reverend Jeff Procter-Murphy. You may recognize these two pastors also as co-creators of the informative and provocative Living the Questions curriculum resources, familiar to Progressive Christian individuals and gatherings around the world. Both have been my pastors, and significant influences in my own evolving journey of faith and understanding.

These Prayers of Via de Cristo first came about through informal collaborations with then pastor, Ken Morrison. During our conversations, he introduced me to the invaluable sense of liturgy as "the work of the people," which has so strongly influenced the content and voice of these works. Written nearly weekly as Calls to Worship, these earlier prayers were first created in call and response form.

As Jeff Procter-Murphy followed Pastor Morrison in the pastorate of Via de Cristo, these prayers evolved into centering prefaces to the sermon time, and into their present reflection-and-prayer form. It was at his quiet insistence, and the encouragement of a number of our congregants, that I began the process of bringing these prayers together in this printed book form.

This creation of these prayers, and the completion of this book, has continued with the encouragement of present Pastor Kristin Longenecker.

Penny Davis, Denise DiCenso, Carol Engle, and Teresa Dubuque were great encouragers, particularly in finding personal and other uses for some of these prayers. Judy Knotts King was immensely helpful in proofing and editorial suggestions. Anything that remains amiss in this regard I freely claim as the result of my subsequent touch-ups of text and format.

I must also acknowledge the very real contributions of the music men who along the way taught and encouraged me and involved me in new journeys into creative writing and visual media that have shaped my spiritual life and stewardship. Thank you Larry Roberts, Gordon Christopher, David Red, and John Shillington.

I am clearly indebted to all of these encouragements, and grateful for the emergence of this nearest thing to a disciplined devotional practice to find its way into my adult life. I am also ever so appreciative of the Provident and Creative Impulse that brings us all together in such a way.

The cover image is used with the kind permission of Mario del Angel.

Dedicated to my wife Myrtle, the patient, smart, and encouraging love of my life, ...game companion and fellow traveller through more than fifty years of marriage.

TABLE OF CONTENTS

FOREWORD

ALL ABOUT US

INNER WORKINGS

SEASONS

SPECIAL CIRCUMSTANCE

ABOUT THE AUTHOR
ENDNOTES

FOREWORD

The prayers gathered in this collection were created for the worship services of Via de Cristo United Methodist Fellowship in North Phoenix/Scottsdale, Arizona.

They are the direct result of our felt need for our Calls to Worship to make more specific connection with our worship service themes and occasions, while at the same time giving voice to the distinctive Progressive Christian character of Via de Cristo UMC.

Throughout these works, you will encounter certain recurring themes and phrases, including our fellowship's shortened name, "Via de Cristo." Among our people, these words are heard not only as our fellowship's name, but also as synonymous with its translation, the Way of Christ. This is a reflection of our desire to be a living invitation to any and all to join us as fellow travelers and explorers in the Way of this Jesus.

Greetings and blessings from a fellow pilgrim, Jim A

ALL ABOUT US

Beatitudes

We have come to call these sayings of Jesus ... the Beatitudes.
Were Jesus a perfumer, these might be essential oils,
the tiny residues extracted from flowers,
yet bearing the full beauty of their floral scent.

But these are the distillations of a teacher,
...Jesus' message of hope and encouragement
offered to a gathering of the curious
on the gentle slopes of a certain Galilean hillside.

The moment,
...filled with his directness and clarity of message,
...was not lost, neither then, nor now.

Divine Presence,
immersed in the realities and conflicts of our own time,
these carefully worded sayings
seem to ask the impossible of us,

...asking that we strive to live in harmless
and benevolent relationship with one another;

...and in doing so,
become the realization of our Creator's
expectations and hope in and for us.

How grateful then we must be
for a Jesus who never seemed to ask for,
nor expect, perfection among his companions,
...even those he called his friends;

...asking only that we walk in constant awareness
of the fragrance of these ideals that adorn our path,
...heeding their call to a better way
...a way we have come to know as the Via de Cristo. – Amen

Craft of Witness[1]

How easily we speak of being *followers* of Jesus,
   ...sometimes of being *imitators* of Christ.
But in a reflective moment, we may ask
    if this is really what Jesus ultimately expected of his chosen disciples,
      and whether this would have been his hope for us in our own day,
        ...for us to be only followers and imitators.

Perhaps Jesus' impatience with his followers,
   ...the urgency that he felt with his disciples,
     ...had something to do with a time quickly approaching
      when these beloved pupils
        would themselves become teachers;
     ...a time when mere imitation would be inadequate
      for those becoming the living heirs
        of Jesus' vision and message;
     ...finding themselves now leaders, instead of followers.

Divine Presence –
   may that moment arrive for us as well,
     ...when we find ourselves no longer followers,
       ...realizing that we too know the way,
        ...this Via de Cristo,
     ...when we no longer have to ask what Jesus would do,
      because we are seeing and feeling
        with the eyes and heart of the Christ.

May we grow in awareness that we too have become living heirs;
   ...heirs of a message not of persuasion,
     but of invitation into Jesus' vision and message,
       ...into the wholeness and justice
        of the living presence of the Christ.

And may our witness to others we encounter
   no longer be in second or third person,
     but in first person present,
       as we reflect the living presence
        of the Christ within us.   – Amen

Voices from the Past

The path of tradition from Jesus to our own time is far from straight,
full of redirections and forks in the road.

How blessed we are
that many who have walked this path before us
left us records of their passing,
...of their understandings and of their ways.

How blessed we are
that some among these also left us personal
and unflinching records of their struggles,
...for among them we find the very names
that mark the turning places of insight and reform
in ourselves, and in our traditions.

Their diversities have blessed us in their many ways
of approaching and living in the presence of the Divine.

Their struggles reassure us in our own questioning,
and learning, and changing;
ultimately speaking to us in our own time of grace,
...of divine grace greater than our missteps,
...of the endowment of grace in the goodness
and bounty of Creation,
...and of learned grace that can adorn our lives,
and quiet the storms for others.

We are indebted to these who speak to us from the past,
...but grateful as well for those in our own time
who even now struggle to create new voices
whose messages of wisdom and grace
may be heard well by those generations
yet to come.   – Amen

Mystics

The voices of the mystics speak to us of intersections with the Divine,
   ...of a kind of knowing that ventures beyond belief,
     ...beyond intellectual understanding,
      ...into "the wild things of God."[2]

They speak of a way of seeing the whole of Creation as single,
   ...as connected,
     ...as an unimaginably expansive woven work
      of peace, and love, and joy beyond description.

Divine Presence,
   you *are*;
     ...and we *are*.

And though we ourselves are creatures in an aviary of time and space,
   ...and you are not,
     ...in some ways beyond our ken,
      still we sense that there is somehow
       an intersection of our ways.

May we learn to listen for the voices of the mystics,
   – the timeless utterances and the new –
     ...speaking to us of contemplation and surrender;
      ...of trust in the deeper, transforming messages
       to be found in the places of wonder,
      ...of creativity,
       ...of compassion and restoration,
        ...even in suffering.

May we learn to create oases of silence,
   ...to seek,
     and to ponder our own encounters with the Divine,
      glimpsed by the mystic within us.

And may we find in their quiet
   the "thin places"[3] that call us away from the man-things
     which distance us from one another,
      ...and from the intent of the Impulse of Creation itself.   – Amen

Greater Things than These

How shall we respond to Jesus telling his disciples
    that they will do works greater than he himself has done?

We are inclined – through our traditions –
    to get lost in thoughts of special empowerments or anointings
        that somehow transformed these followers
            out of their familiar human frailties.

But in these words, Jesus spoke not of empowerment or anointing,
    nor of miracles or supernatural strength,
        …but of simple labors,
        …of human work.

The simplicity of this understanding
    rests so easy with the way of Jesus,
        …seeing everyone through eyes
            that see no class and distinction,
        …releasing these words to flow down to us,
            …to speak directly to us in our own time.

Divine Presence,
    as we hear these words, and chance to look at our own hands,
        may it be that we find hands engaging these greater works,
            filled with the unimaginable tools and knowledge
            of our remarkable time.

As we look to one another – here gathered as brothers and sisters –
    may we see hands laboring together to spread larger and wider yet
        the goodness and privilege you have gifted us in Creation.

And as we look at the hands of our children,
    may we find them discovering ways of carrying
        still greater blessing and healing into generations to come.

May our lives repeat back the words of your Liturgy for us,
    as we learn to do justly,
        …to love mercy,
            …and to walk in gratitude and humility,
                …in your Way we call the Via de Cristo. – Amen

Song Unsung

Though we don't understand exactly how,
    our songs touch us deeply,
        ....speaking to us in ways beyond those
          of any action or spoken word.

Old and new,
    ...infinite in variety and voice,
        our songs speak of joy and sorrow,
          ...draw us into remembrance and celebration,
          ...and bind us into community,
            as we give voice to our awareness
              of God's presence and providence.

Gracious God,
    if our very being is a living song,
        each one unique in all of time and place,
          each with its own potential beyond our imagining,
            ...let us not be a song unsung.

Let us freely put our hands to the work,
    telling our stories, sharing our dreams,
        ...singing our own special song,
          and letting your kingdom bless the earth through us.

And in the rare pauses in life,
    when we are brought to silence and stillness
        before the unfathomable depths of the nighttime skies,
          or at the dayspring of new life,
    ...in that rare moment when we feel a certain powerful feeling
        of joy and awe that aches within us, ...wanting to take flight,
          but beyond the limitations of words or action,
        ...may we recognize it as the song of our heart
          sung in wordless beauty to you.   – Amen

This morning we are particularly mindful of the invisible servants among us,
the many whose labors – both large and small –
are hidden to us,
...behind the scenes.

Some we have chosen for the work to be done.
But others have found their own invisible ways of service,
some during our gathering times,
...still others in times of their own making.

How blessed we are by those who help us work
within the larger framework of our traditions,
...who keep the records and prepare reports,
...who shepherd our finances,
...who lay the groundwork for our future.

How blessed we are as well
by those who dress our worship space each Sunday,
and help shape the sights and sounds of our services;
...by those who arrange things, prepare our communications,
capture images, and send cards,
...by those who set our signs by the roadsides,
...and those who pick up paper and crumbs
that fall to the floor unnoticed by others.

We take notice of you by the shadows of your invisible service.
We know your hearts, and love you for it.

We are what we are through your indispensable gifts,
and richer and better as well, as we are able to follow your example
in this way of being in service to one another,
...in this way of being a part of the Via de Cristo,
...as we understand it,
...and seek to practice it.   – Amen

Welcoming the Stranger

How blessed we are by the presence of those
who come among us for the first time,
...whether just once, or for a season,
or perhaps as a prelude to a longer time of walking,
and talking, ...and serving alongside one another.

Divine Presence,
may all who cross our threshold
encounter hands of greeting and warmth,
...inviting conversation and refreshment,
...and the joy flowing from our shared searchings
for the ways of Jesus in our own time and circumstance.

May we be found a good work in progress,
welcoming all without reservation or judgment,
seeking only the mind and heart and direction of the Christ.

For those who hunger and thirst for a more Christ-shaped
expression of "church," may they find in us kindred souls,
drawn together not to think alike,
but to think *together* on things of importance.

For those healing from hurt or loss,
...or wounded through church failure,
...or perhaps just tired,
...may we be to them a sacred oasis where the water is sweet,
and there is time to rest in the shade and recover.

To those whose explorations into the deeper and harder questions
have elsewhere been discouraged,
may we be found a people who learn
from each other's questions and explorations.

To those whose faith is in flux, evolving from an inherited faith
toward the integrity of a more personal, internal faith walk,
may they find themselves among kindred souls.

And when we part ways, may that sense of kinship linger long,
...an enduring bond among seekers in the Via de Cristo.   – Amen

We are creatures imbued with mystery,
   ...with life and awareness,
      ...with mind and memory,
         ...with curiosity and reason.

In every direction we look,
   ...in every dimension we explore,
      with every discovery we make,
         ...we encounter still yet greater mystery.

And just beyond these lie the grand mysteries:
   ...the beginnings of being,
      ...the Author and Activator of all that is,
         ...and our place in the unfolding of this Creation.

We gather here this morning as seekers of our place in this unfolding.

We are a people of shared faith because we have experienced
   the remarkable habit of Creation to reveal more of itself,
      – and of its Author – as we grow ready.

We are a like-minded people because the Via de Cristo we have chosen
   continues to provoke and affirm us in finding new ways to recognize
      and honor the divine imprint within us,
         ...even as our understanding evolves.

We gather in this place because our tradition invites us
   into these intersections of mystery and discovery.

Holy Presence,
   ...may we continue to find new ways
      of turning our point of reference inside out,
   ...new ways of drawing aside the curtains of man-proclaimed mystery
      until we recognize that divine signature in *all* we encounter,
         ...woven into the everyday, ...and into every new thing,
      ...until we recognize it as a sign of affection
        for all who walk with us in this small,
           sacred corner of the universe. – Amen

Nothing Is Ordinary

By the works of creation, we recognize the architect.[4]
    And if we but take notice,
        the movements of this Creation *invite* us to explore,
           introducing us to layer upon layer
               of new understanding and new meaning;
               yet always greater mystery remaining;
                  ...always wonder and awe.

Author of All That Is –
    we once thought that only *this thing*, or *that place*,
        ...or *that way*, ...was sacred.

But we have come to know that You *were*, when the universe was not;
    ...that you alone attended the mystery of beginnings
        forged in a fire of heat beyond knowing,
    ...imagining an elegance of complexities flowing from simplicities,
        ...of immensity that refashions the impossible into possible,
        ...of purest energy transforming into substance,
        ...of dust clouds and stars, and their cycles,
        ...of earths, ...and waters, ...and seasons,
        ...of the evolutions of life,
           ...and of a place for us.

We once thought *this* was all about *us*.
    But now we are finding that the whole of divine purpose
        is not met in us alone.
And yet, here we are,
    ...in this one out-of-the-way, delicately balanced place
        in the enormity of this evolving creation,
           ...and there is work for us here that is uniquely ours.

And from this place, we are seeing more and more
    of the sacred in the ordinary,
        ...even learning to *be* the sacred within the ordinary.

Perhaps in time, we will see that there *is no* ordinary,
    ...for every part of what we are now
        was present in that first instant of Creation.
    So where can we stand
        and not be a holy thing on holy ground? – Amen

The Next Step

How fortunate we are to live in such a time,
   ...as beings so complex of body and mind,
      ...and offered an unprecedented spectrum
         of new opportunities among our kind and kin.

But greater opportunities have also brought greater challenges.
   Many have become portals into new insights and understanding,
      ...into new avenues of healing and restoration,
        ...into new ways living in community,
           ...even refining and reshaping our sense of the Divine.

Some are daunting, and seemingly insurmountable.
   Some new, ...some timeless, ...catch us in mid-flight in life,
     and bring us abruptly to ground, ...even to an absolute stop,
      stalled in uncertainty, indecision and frustration.

Giver of life, and all that blesses and nurtures it,
   we gather in gratitude this morning
     for those who have helped us understand that at such times,
      a single next step can unlock the journey
        into the rest of our lives.

We gather in gratitude for those who have offered direction,
   ...who have invited us into an abiding faith
    that allows us to step out when we must;
   ...who invited us into a faith that displaces fear
    when the way is distressing or unclear.

   ...in gratitude for the rich and varied experiences of life
    that quietly morph into wisdom for the journey ahead,
   ...in gratitude for all that earlier sustained and nurtured us,
    yet now recedes behind us.
   ...in gratitude for the richness of companionship and community
    that taught us of grace and love,
      ...of wisdom and compassion, ...of hope and resilience,
     ...and all else that sustains us
      as we draw in our breath,
        ...to take the next step.   – Amen

Wildflowers

Are we not somehow akin to wildflowers strewn on the mountain slopes,
    born of the earth, metamorphosed from the latency of seeds
        into living, growing, and blossoming things;
            …nurtured by one and the same soil, rain, and sunshine,
              …yet maturing in beauty,
                  and diversities of color and shape and size and place?

Still, we are wildflowers that have awakened
    to something beyond mere being,
        …beyond doing a single thing that is our lot in life.

We are wildflowers awakened to the wonder of ourselves,
    …to the wonder of our surroundings;
        …to dreaming and creating, to sharing love and compassion,
            even to pondering of meanings, and the why of our being.

We are wildflowers freed from the soil to move about,
    choosing to gather into gardens,
        or to give ourselves away;
            …sadly, even to allow ourselves to wither and die
              in uselessness and neglect.

In all our otherness,
    still we can learn from the wildflowers on the mountainside
        who quietly bask in the bounty and providence of Creation;
        genuine and harmless and faithful in who they are;
        oblivious to the differences among their kind,
            generous with their beauty,
              …and when the time comes to depart,
                leaving a legacy of life for another season.

We could do worse than that.   – Amen

'Treasures

If our eyes were truly clear for just a moment,
   and if we were asked in that very moment
      to hold out our hands before the provident God of Creation,
  we might see revealed in one hand
     a dynamic and brilliantly colored thing that is our "now,"
       …the living and breathing present
         formed of the entangled fibers of our lives,
           …of our substance, and our relationships,
            …and of what we are doing with them.

In our other hand rests a cloudier thing,
   …a more diaphanous interweaving of divine hope and human dreams,
  and the possibilities in what we might build toward the future.

Divine Presence,
  we are in growing awareness that in your Creation,
    the living portions of these "nows,"
      …and the "yet to comes,"
        have been placed in our hands,
         …unreservedly, …expectantly,
          …ours to shape, whether by intent or neglect.

So may their shapings at our hands be by intent, …even by vision.

May we see the "nows" and the "yet to comes,"
   …as formative and living treasures in our hands.

And may our husbanding of them be
   not out of tradition, …or obligation or guilt,
     …but because the building of something that matters now,
       …and matters to the future before us,
        …has captured our imaginations,
        and our hearts.   – Amen

First Wonder

Surely it must have been the stars in the night sky
    that first caused us to wonder,
        …mysterious in their beauty, …in their constancy,
          …in their tantalizing patterns and scintillations,
            …moving in their majestic and ordered ways.

How could one not reflect deeply on what they might be,
    …and wonder about that something so much greater than ourselves
        that must have placed them there.

In our own time, we have been given eyes that see ever further
    and deeper into the wonders and workings of this creation,
        …given ways of seeing what our eyes alone cannot see,
          …going where our eyes cannot go,
            …and thinking of what lies still further yet
              in the darkness of the unknown.

And so, …we stand in that same timeless awe,
    …every layer of awareness and understanding
        revealing new beauty within beauty, …direction within disorder,
      …simplicities within complexities, …creations within Creation.
And yet always more remains just out of reach,
    …still more yet beyond human knowing.

Gracious God,
    we sense too the Mystery beyond the mysteries.
      We sense something of you in the brushstrokes of the sunset,
        and the music of the waters;
      …hear you in songs of the woodlands and the whale,
      …see you in the workings of the cosmos and the stem cell,
      …and feel your presence as we explore
        the continuing revelations of the stars,
        …and of the stones of the earth.

Even our own gifts of curiosity, imagination, and creativity,
    seem only reflections of the mystery that is you.
      Our prayer is that we safeguard and nurture them well
        in our brief sojourn here,
          …as we build a legacy for those who follow us,
          …as we share in establishing your kingdom
            …here on Earth. – Amen

In Our Hands

If we but have eyes to see, mystery surrounds us.
  Some invites us to exploration, and pondering,
    to discovery and understanding ...if only a layer at a time.
      But some is different, ...and deep ...beyond our knowing.

Mystery swirls about our very being.
  Even as we call ourselves "beings"
    much of what we are and how we work remains unknown.
      Even the very wondering of who and what we are is mystery.

We are drawn in fruitful curiosity toward the smaller mysteries,
  ...yet brought to our knees before the deepest ones.

Mystery of Mysteries,
  may it be that we neither lose nor diminish
    our sense of mystery and wonder.

May we ever be in awe of the workings and unfoldings of the cosmos,
  and the greater Mystery that put them in place.
May we remain in awe of life, and beauty;
  ...in awe of our places as moving parts in such a creation,
    even though we cannot know the whole of its workings;
  ...in awe that, in us, creature has become creator,
    ...and healer, ...and restorer,
      ...and doer of a thousand good things that only mankind,
        among all other of Earth's creatures, can do.

As the mystery of our work in this place continues to unfold,
  we are realizing more and more that the stewardship of *all this*
    has been entrusted into *our* hands.

We are awestruck, ...taken by surprise, ...deeply humbled,
  ...and a little afraid.   – Amen

Husbanding Creation

Gracious God,
    you scattered the possibilities of us coming into being,
        like seeds thrust into the fertile soil
            of your unimaginably vast creation.
Perhaps you watched,
      ...and waited through the long, lifeless winter,
        ...until we burst forth, a living kind,
          born of the earth, full of new possibility,
        ...knowing a little, imagining much,
        ...thinking ourselves the near-culmination of Creation's great plan.

In the warmth of your providence we basked,
    drawing from the earth what we needed,
        ...and what we wanted to sustain us, and amuse us,
          ...taking little notice of the needs of our earth-garden.

Of late, though, we have taken to the air
    like silken-winged seeds in the wind,
      lifted higher, seeing further,
         ...finding ourselves growing smaller
          among the mysteries unfolding before us.

Did you smile in your own way as we discovered ours was an island-garden,
    ...circling a single star amongst a hundred million more,
      ...pale blue, ...daubed with the browns of our living places,
        ...whorled with the whiteness
          of our world's life-sustaining mists?

Did you lean in closer as we began to see everything about us
    as finely interwoven,
      ...and in delicately balanced need
        of every other thing on this earth?
    ...as it began to dawn on us that we are the husbandmen
      of this gifted place,
        ...of the whole of our island-garden, and all that grows in it?

May we now grow in wisdom,
    ...into our newfound roles in this always-changing world,
      ...seeking balance between knowing and humility,
        ...between privilege and gratitude,
          ...as we labor to prepare a still better place
            of providence and beauty
              for generations and possibilities yet to come.   – Amen

Hope of Creation

Out of some unknowable emptiness and chaos,
　　our dwelling place was slowly breathed into being,
　　　　…the mountains that punctuate the plains,
　　　　　　…the rivers that course through its valleys,
　　　　　　　　…and the vastness of the oceans – earth's pulsing heart.

Wind and rain, …and fire and flood,
　　the constant agents of change and newness,
　　　　…and the swaths of green that contend with the deserts,
　　　　　　…they all beckoned us.

And so too came creature life,
　　small and large, sensing, and even thinking,
　　　　finding ever new ways to accept the hospitalities
　　　　　　and possibilities of this diverse and life-giving place.

And then man, …a new kind, …curious and imagining,
　　…dreaming of what might be,
　　…and able to bend slightly the will and movement
　　of all that came before,
　　　　…creating whole new paths and new dwelling places.

Surely, woven through this wondrous fabric of creation
　　are the Creator's own dreams,
　　　　golden threads of hope, ….of justice, and compassion,
　　　　　　…and the uninterrupted flow of peace among these
　　　　　　who somehow bear a mark of the Creator,
　　　　　　　　…who perhaps even carry within an ember
　　　　　　　　or a wisp of transcendent presence.

And so, today, Gracious God,
　　we celebrate the wonder of being set free,
　　　　…to choose our paths in this daring adventure of trust,
　　　　…and to celebrate the promise of what might yet come to be
　　　　through our thoughts …and words,
　　　　　　through our actions, …and our collaborations.

May our spiritual reflections together
　　bring new shape to our todays, …and our tomorrows,
　　　　as our lives move toward the truest form of worship,
　　　　　　…drawn by a force as gentle, yet insistent as gravity,
　　　　　　　　into coursing streams of faith, …and love,
　　　　　　　　　　…the living expressions of divine hope.　 – Amen

Seasons (Sarah)

How well we know the rhythms of the seasons,
 ...the tender greens of spring,
  ...the rains of summer,
   ...the colors of autumn,
    ...and the deep slumber of winter.

Abraham's beloved Sarah marked their comings and goings as well,
 even as they stretched into the seasons of her life,
  ...her spring of anticipation,
   ...her summer of warmth and waiting still,
    ...her autumn of waning hope,
     ...and her winter of childless sorrow and resignation.

Holy Presence,
 in the ebb and flow of seasons in our lives, we are much like Sarah.

In our springs of anticipation,
 ...we have reveled in your gifts of joy and new possibility.

In our summers, we have basked in a sense of your nearness,
 ...in the way of old friends on long, wordless walks together.

In the autumns of our lives, as uncertainties loomed on the horizon,
 ...we have reached out to you for reassurance and calm.

And in our winters, when disappointment and loss sojourned with us,
 ...when we have felt ourselves somehow distanced,
  ...we were seekers once again of the solace and sanctuary
  we have found only in you.

Gracious God,
 even now as we still our hearts in your presence,
  we long to grow into more abiding awareness
   of your constancy and nearness
    ...as moment flows into moment,
     ...and season into season.

Even so, may we
 ...like Sarah,
  ...be inclined to laughter
   should surprise find us in winter. – Amen

On This Rock

This morning we speak of the foundation of the church,
　　the core vision that shapes who we are and what we do
　　　　as a people of God.

Though we build not with stone,
　　we have nonetheless come together in this place to build,
　　　　...to give life to that vision.

Gracious God,
　　we acknowledge in this moment the privilege
　　　　of entering into the time just ahead in our church's life.

As we put our hands to this work, may we craft it with care,
　　...making sure that everything needful is done,
　　　　...and to the best of our abilities.

May we approach it with courage,
　　...reaching beyond comfort
　　　　to make the most of the moments in our hands.

And may we anticipate,
　　...finding joy in building as others before us,
　　　　...in preparation for those of like mind and heart
　　　　　　yet to follow.

May the world immediately about us
　　become more inclined to compassion, and loving-kindness,
　　　　...and to a deeper faith walk simply because we have built here,
　　　　　　...because we bring life to a vision,
　　　　　　　　...and to a way that truly touches people
　　　　　　　　　　and changes lives.   – Amen

Vision

"Vision" can mean the imagining of a future that is ours to bring about,
    through the stewardship of what has been given uniquely to us,
        …in this place,
        …and in this time.

Gracious God,
    ours is not a vision of cathedrals of glass, nor vast numbers,
      nor worldwide visibility.

Ours is a more modest vision,
    …of a people who become known for supporting one another
    in their individual spiritual walks,
        …of a people who favor conversation over conformity,
        "doing" over dogma,
          and direction over destination,
      …as we walk together in the Jesus way,
        …the Via de Cristo.

We envision being known as an evolving gathering,
    …a place where we can adjust our understandings and actions,
      moving toward lives of greater service, meaning, and satisfaction.

We envision being known as a place of open hearts,
    open minds, and open doors,
      …a place that welcomes all,
        …accepting, loving, exploring,
        and sharing our varied spiritual journeys
        with openness and anticipation.

And, we envision being known as a place of transformation,
    where we work together to touch and change the lives and potential
    of those in difficult circumstance.

May it be so, in growing realization of this vision,
    …born of our acknowledgment
      and appreciation of your gifts to us and in us,
May it be so through growing insight and inspiration
    as we continue to contemplate how best to care for
      and nurture one another,
May it be so in the future that we are called
    to bring about in this place. – Amen

INNER WORKINGS

Choices

In our early faith walks, comfort and security were our companions.

But as the faith within us moves and grows,
    we find its way marked by choices that stretch us,
        ...some gently,
            ...others challenging and risky,
                ...and occasionally painful.

Gracious God,
    even so, we choose to live our worship,
        to honor you moment by moment
            by embracing our questions and histories,
                ...our passions and uncertainties,
                ...embracing them not out of habit or obligation,
                    ...but by choice.

And we choose to rethink church,
    in search of a more uncluttered and essential Christianity,
        ...in search of ways of living and being and doing
            that echo more perfectly the heart and message of Jesus.

And in those ways, we choose to help rebuild lives,
    as our way of being your hands of healing
        and restoration and redemption,
            ...extended to our brothers and sisters.

Speak ever in your gentle way to our hearts, even today,
    as we stumble over the questions,
        ...probe our understandings,
            ...and reexamine our ways.

And in the Via de Cristo,
    may we become a living invitation to all,
        ...an invitation into the Via de Cristo,
            ...and into the welcoming presence of the Divine. – Amen

Doubt

In our faith walks, shall we dare to doubt?

Shall we be free to question the roadmaps and markers,
    to weigh our understandings of Scripture's stories and teachings,
        ...even to examine anew the foundations of the faith
            given to us in earlier years?
    Are we in danger of losing the way by questioning the way?

We hear the voice of sacred text saying,
    "Test all things. Hold fast to what is good."

But how shall we test the important things of life, and death, and eternity,
    ...of goodness and truth and purpose,
        ...without the questions?

Is not this thing of doubt surely just another hue
    among the shades of life's ever-changing palette of questions?

Divine Presence,
    we were created in this way of pondering, testing, and learning,
        ...wondrously able to grow in understanding
            and wisdom and service.

And these questions – perhaps especially these we name as doubt –
    ...these questions are surely the sieve
        through which a faith, once given to us by others,
            must pass to become our own.

So may we not shrink from the questions,
    ...trusting you as the wellspring of curiosity, ...and reason,
        ...and our questions.

And may we be unhurried in doubt,
    that certain itch that just won't quite go away,
        recognizing it as our patient teacher.
    May we remain open-minded and open-hearted,
        ...seeking only the integrity of the Way of the Christ,
            ...perhaps leaving behind the easier walk for the better walk,
                ...in the Via de Cristo.　– Amen

Questioning Belief

We are creatures who cannot walk through life without beliefs,
...these speculations that allow us to stitch together
some of the scattered fragments
of our own experience and understandings,
...creating life-tapestries with order and meaning.

We need these beliefs to be able to live and move
in a creation we cannot fully understand,
...to live and move in the presence and providence
of divinity that is a greater mystery yet.

And so Gracious God,
how blessed we are that the wisdom and counsel of Scripture
is to test all things,
... to even allow our own beliefs to be tested,
...and then to hold fast to what is good.

How freeing it is to know that our beliefs may change
in the light of circumstance, and shared experience,
...and as we wrestle over time
with some of the deeper questions of faith,
...as some beliefs weaken and fall away,
and as a few transform into foundation stones
for a more mature and abiding faith.

May we be courageous when questions lead us into uncertainty,
...patient when we're not even sure what questions to ask,
...and gentle as we give ourselves permission
to revisit the beliefs of our earlier years,
...in order to find that more perfect way
of following the footsteps
of the one called Jesus,
in the way we call the Via de Cristo.   – Amen

Prayer

There is a certain familiar stillness in such moments as this,
   …this time of prayer.
Even as we set aside the busyness and concerns
   and routines that otherwise occupy us,
      our sacred writings bid us, "Be still and know."

… And so in these moments, we welcome the quiet,
   … setting free our circles of thought,
      … inviting that curious quieting of soul
         that wakens to the presence of Spirit.
      …that speaks more eloquently
         of the presence of Spirit
            than the finest of words.

Holy Presence,
   This … practice of prayer, …this very impulse to pray
      remains among the great mysteries of our faith.

Our traditions have taught us much about how we might pray,
   …yet we waver in thinking of you as parent or patriarch,
      …as sister or sovereign,
         …as companion, …or ineffable.
         May we be still, …and just … know.

Our traditions have taught us much about how we might pray,
   …but much remains so exquisitely personal
      that we must find our own way.
         May we be still, …and know.

Our traditions have taught us much about how we might pray,
   …but there is no one who can teach us the wordless,
      inexpressible prayer we feel rise up within us in your presence.
         …Somehow, we already know this song.   – Amen

Wrestling

This morning we think together about certain times of inner struggle
    encountered in our faith walks,
        …introspective times when we find ourselves with one foot
          on the familiar ground of what we've always thought,
            what we've been taught, …how we've understood,
             and the beliefs we've shared;
       …yet our other foot rests tentatively
          on the untested footing of new insight,
            or perhaps diversities of understanding
             that do not rest easy, …even conflict
               with some of what we've trusted as bedrock.

And so we contend with questions that we can no longer ignore.
    Some have long been our companions;
    some only intermittent visitors;
     …still others have been thrust suddenly into our consciousness
      by some circumstance.

But they have this in common:
    though we may put them on hold for a time,
      these questions don't go away.

Giver of life, and all that it blesses,
    it seems it's not the path you have called us to in life,
      to seek the easy answers and shortcuts that float on the surface,
       …to remain oblivious to the deeper uncertainties just below.

So may we welcome the questions and the struggles,
    …making time for the sacred process of testing our certainties,
    …pondering deeply what is right, and true, and important.

May we cultivate patience,
    …being neither too quick,
      nor yet too slow to allow change in our inner selves,
       …as we are ready.

May we remain in wonder always
    at our ability to wrestle with things of importance.

And may integrity and a still-growing faith mark our way
    as we embrace the restiveness of the struggles
      in the Via de Cristo. – Amen

Living Waters

We have known the desert around us.
  We gather – here in this coolness –
    as refugees from the withering heat that surrounds us.
We crave the coolness of the mists,
  and the scent of the rains that bring the miracle of life to the desert.

We have known, too, the deserts of life.
  As we enter this space, we try to whisk away – for a moment –
    …the dry and abrasive tumult of daily life,
      …the neediness, and demands,
        …and routines that seem to dam up
          the calming waters of divine presence.
  We thirst for your nearness, O God, and for quiet interludes of retreat.

We have known the deserts of the soul,
  when your waters of deep peace seem so distant,
    …so silent,   …a mirage.
      We are desolate and withered without you.

  But you have offered us *living* waters.
    You speak of them flowing *out* of us.

Gracious, patient, forgiving, healing, restoring, life-giving God,
  we are so thirsty for this living water.
    We would know anew the flow of rivers of forgiveness,
      the splash of the inexhaustible spring of love,
        the calm of the still waters,
          and the quiet cleansing of the rains
            that speak of your presence.

Help us this very day to make a fresh resolve, to drink daily
  – even moment by moment – of the living water you offer us.

Bind us as one family to draw deeply,
  our vessels overflowing as we search out the dry places,
    …and the arid souls,
      …becoming for them new springs of living water.   – Amen

About God

This morning, we come together as always
  from many directions, …many life paths.
And yet in these few moments,
    through the quieting of our minds and hearts,
      we approach a profound oneness,
        a shared sense of presence and connection
          with something greater, …much greater, than ourselves.

We have used "Spirit" to name this something,
    …whose unfolding Creation made a way and a place for the likes of us.
    "God," we say, in a hundred ways, in ten thousand tongues.

But how often we use these names to somehow claim ownership
    of Spirit that cannot be owned, …to address Spirit that needs no name.

We human kind have thought of Spirit sometimes as one, …and many.
    Yet, number may be without meaning to Spirit
      who *was* before there were things to count,
        who *was* before there was a *before*.

We have imagined Spirit as dwelling unseen in the winds, and the forests,
    and the creatures that inhabit them,
      …or dwelling beyond our reach in the heights of the mountains,
        or depths of volcanoes;
      …or further yet, enthroned just beyond
        the star-strewn crystalline dome of the night-time sky.

But then the yet-unfolding revelation of Creation whispers to us,
    "Spirit needs no place. Spirit *is*."

And so we feel we are not alone as we quietly wonder
    if we are observed with eyes we cannot ken,
      …listened to with ears beyond our knowing,
    …not alone as we consider whether curiosity and creativity,
      compassion and love,
        might be more than a reflection of Spirit within us.

Perhaps it is instead a certain oneness with Spirit we feel,
    …a oneness of a kind that we have only begun to know.

"Welcome," we say to such encounters;
    even in our uncertainties and our wonderings, …"Welcome!"   – Amen

Child Again (Faith)

How it resonates with something deep inside us
    when we hear the laughter of children,
        …when we see their uninhibited movement to music,
            …and their gleeful abandon in playing sprinkler games.

We smile, …even laugh with them,
    …because part of ourselves once knew very well
        those exuberant and carefree ways.

But now there seems to be another part of us
    that knows too much of other ways,
        …a more bruised, …and experienced,
        …and cautious part of us
            that often prefers to watch
                and enjoy from the safety of the sidelines.

Holy Presence,
    is it possible that we live unnecessarily in tension
        between these two parts of ourselves,
        …between the part of us that wants to throw caution
            to the wind, and go for it,
        …and the part of us that now knows all too well
            the unpleasant and even painful dimensions
                of risk and consequence?

Surely our possibilities are greater now than when we were children.
Surely the experience, and insight, and understanding
    that ushered us into adulthood, and into the strength of community
    does not speak to us of sidelines,
        …but of new possibilities, …and new fulfillments.

May we then remember again how to launch ourselves without reserve,
    trusting in the rightness and worthwhileness
        of what we are setting out to do;
        …choosing these directions despite the risks,
        …leaving behind only the naive bliss of childhood;
            …and calling this new thing "faith."

May we – in this new way – find that child part of us again,
    …going for it with all the joys and possibilities of our real selves,
        …right here, …right now, …in the Via de Cristo.   – Amen

Change

Shouldn't we all be people of music?
    Shouldn't we
        – who somehow bear your likeness and live in your Creation –
          be able to move and glide effortlessly
            through the jostlings and twists and turns
              of life's events and circumstance?

Even as we call you Gracious God,
    we acknowledge you as the wellspring of grace for such moments.

So when the music changes,
    may we learn to greet it with a sense of fresh possibility,
        embracing both the necessary and the unexpected
          with anticipation, …and hope.

When the key changes,
    may we know whether to sing melody,
        …accompany,
          …or simply lend our movement to the music.

When we ourselves rewrite the music,
    may grace notes abound,
        …perfectly shaped, and perfectly placed.

And may we, in time, learn to embrace
    both the overtures and finales of circumstance,
        recognizing every "now" as simply the chrysalis
          for the new thing we are always becoming.

Help us learn to sing every song,
    …to dance every dance,
        …to embrace every new turn in life
          with grace that flows from the reassuring constancy
           of your presence in and through us. – Amen

Orbits

How shall we be, "In the world, but not of the world"?
　　How shall the mind of Christ be in us?

Gracious God,
　　these seem so beyond reach as we are pulled to and fro
　　　　by the conflicting forces and distractions of everyday life.

Still, we feel something of you within us that calls us toward a better way.

Our hearts yearn to surrender more fully to your unwavering attraction,
　　...so that we may rise above the stable orbits of the ordinary,
　　　　toward your finer vision for us.

So our simple prayer
　　– even as we enter this gathering time –
　　　　is that the transforming work of this Via de Cristo
　　　　　　continue within us until this better way
　　　　　　　　...until this way, and our own way, become one.

May our hearts and minds and doors be always open.
　　May we constantly seek new ways to touch people and change lives.

And may we be ever mindful of your call toward the "better"
　　that lies just beyond the "good" of the present.　　– Amen

Mustard Seed

Once again we encounter the mustard seed among Jesus' teachings.
 And are we not ourselves a little like a mustard seed?
  Do we not come into the world tiny, potent with possibility,
   but our course not yet charted?

The tiny mustard seed, scattered by the hand of a farmer,
  may also be caught up in a passing breeze,
   …even as the courses of our own lives are shaped,
    sometimes by intent, sometimes by winds of circumstance.

And so, Gracious God,
  in this way, and in so many others,
   Jesus' message of the mustard seed still speaks to us,
    …and still challenges us.

Our faith germinated in the simple soil of childhood nurture and trust.
But as we drew in nourishment, …and drove down roots,
  and unfolded our first leaves,
   we found a brightly lit, opportunity laden,
    yet less innocent and naive world.
   …And we discovered choice, …and distractions.

And so we ask today, "Have we pushed on as we could,
  …more leaves, …more blossoms,
   …more faith-seeds for a new generation?

Do we push on yet, beyond our thresholds of certainty and safety?
  …shrinking back neither from things new,
   nor from things known all too well.

And does the fruit of our faith delight the palate, …or heal?
  …Or does it go unnoticed?

May our faith grow with purpose, as a seed in the hand,
  …and not a seed in the winds of chance;

And may we ask what greater thing faith can lead us to do,
  now that we have discovered
   how to move mountains with our hands.   – Amen

Spirit-Soil

How beautifully the Bible, …our scripture, …our wisdom book,
    …speaks of us at times as living plant-things,
        growing and flowering and bearing fruit.

But one of Jesus' teachings ventures deeper,
    …into a kindred image, but likening us instead to the soil itself,
        the patient, quietly present and benevolent host,
            fostering the plant's germination,
                …nurturing its growth,
                    …and its steady movement toward a fruitful maturity.

Gracious and provident God,
    what a peculiar soil we are, … having hands, and hearts, and minds.

May it be that the roots of Scripture's wisdom and truths
    grow deep and strong in us as one, and as a garden-community.
May they grow in us into living testimony to the presence
    and the providence of the one who is the Author of All That Is.

May the work of our hands loosen the soil.
    May our hearts warm it,
        …and our minds clear it of those habits, and expectations,
            and judgments, and distractions
                that litter and constrain and choke.

Still, may we be patient, …with ourselves, and with others, as we learn,
    …as we process the questions,
        …as we ponder our own experiences and uncertainties,
            and the incompleteness and imperfections of what we are.

In all, may we remain ever mindful of the Bringer of Life,
    as we strive to enrich this soil that we are,
        as we walk together yet a little further in the Via de Cristo.   – Amen

Distractions

We are a people gathered together today in this place,
  ...and in this fellowship,
    ...because we have all heard in some way
      the voice of the one named Jesus,
        calling us to a higher way of living
          both before our Creator,
            ...and in our ways among all others.

And yet there are these distractions,
  ...distractions that seem to set us in conflict with one another,
    dividing us,
      ...and diverting our attention and energies away
        from the simple way of this Jesus.

The words of the Letter to the Galatians enquire,
  "Having started with the Spirit, are you now ending with the flesh?"[5]

Gracious God,
  in this particular day in the life of Via de Cristo,
    may we be reminded that we have freely chosen the way of Christ;
   ...reminded that in the Via de Cristo,
    "There is no longer Jew or Greek,
      there is no longer slave or free,
        there is no longer male and female;
          for *all* are one in Christ Jesus.[6]"

In following the way of this Jesus, may we remember always
  that there is no "them,"
    ...there is no "they";
      ...that in the Via de Cristo there is only "we"
        ...and You. – Amen

Emergence

We feel so comfortable in our ruts,
    with their familiar directions and bounds.
        And it takes much to jar us out of them.

But once in a great while, there is a certain growing restlessness,
    …something unsatisfied or unrealized within us
        that seeks new direction.

It quietly asks for a pause,
    …a small break in the routine
        to reflect on what we are about,
            …and how we are going about it.

Gracious God,
    some of us may be in search of a new vision.
        May we see our work as the building of hope and heritage,
            ….of opportunity and refuge,
                …as expanding our understanding
                    of what you ask of us,
                        …and hope for in us.

Some of us may feel drawn toward a new balance point
    between give and take in our church life.
        May anticipation grow within us as we think anew
            about our gifts and abilities in a community way,
                …so that no job remains undone,
                  …no broken thing unfixed,
                    …and no opportunity unexplored.

Surely, churches can do nothing without the feet and hands and minds
    of those who love and serve together in fellowship.
So may we think generously and expectantly
    as we set about the work of building community,
        …rebuilding lives,
            …and creating a living legacy of faith for our children,
                …and for our successors,
            …even as you have shown us
                through the life of the one we know as Jesus. – Amen

Gracious God,
    as we enter this moment, all is not well with your world,
      …and all is not well with the body of Christ.

We are mindful of a baptismal vow we exchange in our tradition,
    …to "resist evil, injustice and oppression
      in whatever forms they present themselves. [7]"
    Though ever-present, you call us to push back against these,
      …to hold them at bay.

A peaceful world may be beyond hope,
    ….but it is not beyond action.

A perfect church may be beyond hope,
    …but it is not beyond action.

A perfect us,
    …a perfect me,
      …may be beyond hope,
        …but we are not beyond action.

Spirit of Truth,
    may these vows we exchange flow faithfully into what we teach,
      …into what we practice,
        …and into what we are becoming,
      ….as you light our ways
        to "resist evil, injustice and oppression
          in whatever forms they present themselves." – Amen

Being "It"

Chaos seems to somehow have a voice of its own.
    Whether spilled dominoes, loss of leadership, or a tornado's aftermath,
        there's something that calls us to find a way to fix it.

Perhaps it's the small voice somewhere deep within our being
    that knows about the good that can sometimes be rebuilt
      out of disruption and disorder;
        …the same voice that once in a while says,
          "Ready or not, Tag! You're It!"

Gracious God,
    against such a moment, there is much to recognize and appreciate.

We can rejoice as humankind,
    …blessed with remarkable resilience,
      and with the ability to imagine, restore, repair, heal,
        and soften the edges of the hard things.

We can rejoice in our individualities,
    …blessed with diversity,
      contributing to each new situation
        our unique collections of experience, gifts, and insights.

We can also rejoice in community,
    …blessed through the strength of a chosen kinship
      that can sometimes even bring into being
        that which has never existed before.

May we always be receptive to being "It"
    – whether as individuals or in community –
      …bringing into action all that we have been created to be,
        …when that still small voice speaks our name. – Amen

Private Hells

We have come together once again this morning as Via de Cristo.
This very name we gather around speaks of the way of Jesus.

In the moments ahead, we will be pondering what it means
to follow the call and example of Jesus
into the dark places and desolations of life.

These are the private hells all about us, of sickness and death,
of privation and ruin, of misery and loss,
of violence and loneliness, anxiety and fear.
...And we are called to engage them all.

Gracious God,
though these stir our own fears and inadequacies,
we recognize that in your Creation
we are trusted and gifted like no other part of Creation,
to enter into such places in the Way of Jesus,
...bringing warmth against the cold, and sustenance to the hungry
...preventing disease, and walking against injustice
...communing with the outcast,
...comforting the lonely and frightened,
...being quietly present in grief or loss,
...aiding in recovery from the worst that man and nature can inflict.

May we not shrink back
when the Via de Cristo leads into the flames of these private hells.

May our brothers and sisters find in us
that same living presence that sustains us,
should those dark places and desolations be our own.

Help us to do this.
Help us to be this one, ...and this people,
...who know how to walk alongside,
...in this Via de Cristo. – Amen

Starting Anew

It's back to the drawing board
  ...starting from scratch, ...again!

Something didn't work out,
  ...lying broken in pieces,
    ...or no longer working the way it used to.

And suddenly we're not where we were yesterday.
  ...What got us to this day will not carry us into tomorrow.

There is no chart for these waters,
  and yet the approaching tomorrow rests uneasily in our hands.

Gracious God,
  in these moments, we would prefer training wheels,
    rather than the wobbles and crashes of making our own way.
      Yet, we know somehow that this task of tomorrow is ours to do.

In this very moment, we acknowledge our need
  to draw always more deeply from the stability of your purpose in us,
    ...and your presence with us,
      ...and your hope for us.

When there is a place of turning, but the path is not clear,
  may we learn to strike out anew, however daunting that first step.

Where there are only pieces to be picked up,
  ...may we learn to seek a new mosaic, a new work, a new vision.

When tired or discouraged,
  ...may we learn to rest a moment,
    ...catch our breath,
      ...then move on to our next place of service and opportunity,
        ...and learning.

Unchanging One,
  we are ever mindful that whatever changes
    – our world, our circumstances, or even ourselves –
      you are a constant presence,
        ...and your vision of hope our source of strength,
          ...especially when our heading is changing
            to a different tomorrow.   – Amen

Life Laid Down

The words are familiar:
 "Greater love hath no man than this,
  that a man lay down his life for his friends."[8]

Was Jesus speaking of himself?
 ...Or to his disciples who had laid aside their livelihoods
  – all that they knew – when Jesus called them?
   ...Are we called to lay down our own lives?

This has been such a heartrending week,
 with the continuing carnage in the Middle East,
  the specter of disease in Africa,
   the streets of Ferguson awash in fear and outrage.

Gracious God,
 we have heard it said
  that the true measure of love is taken in the hard places.

In this imperfect world, may our voices be heard,
 and our resistance felt wherever injustice and violence reigns.
  May peacemaking, and sanctuary, and healing be our stock and trade,
   in our world, ...and in our backyards.

May our love be courageous should we be called
 to lay down a dream of accomplishment and recognition
  for a life of self-giving service, ...to care for another.

May our love be warm and present when we are called
 to lay down a well-planned day to comfort a grieving friend.

May our love be instant when we are called
 to lay down the urgencies of the moment
  for a few minutes of needed conversation with a child.
   ...else how shall our young know of this kind of love,
    ...constant, ...accessible, ...and selfless.

Author of All That Is,
 how grateful we are for the gift of love,
  ...the miracle of love, ...in all its multifold dimensions.

May this Jesus-kind of love be spread generously,
 and ever more selflessly *through us*
  as we walk in the Way, ...in this Via de Cristo. – Amen

Without Walls

This morning we speak of walls not crafted of brick or stone,
  but those mostly invisible walls that crisscross our lives,
    shaping much of how we apportion the living of our lives
      among others of our kind who share the world with us.

As many other followers of Christ have done,
  we have become more intentional
    about ministering outside the confines of our gathering places
      to touch those in need, …in some ways, …and in some places.

But Spirit of Unity, we confess that so many other barriers remain,
  …quietly detouring us from the way of this one called Jesus.
We build walls of separateness so easily, even unconsciously,
  between people, and institutions, and nations.
And though we surely need some boundaries to survive, …and to thrive,
  …there are so many others that unnecessarily constrain us,
    …but go unchallenged.

This Jesus offers us a way,
  seemingly having dismantled so many of his own walls;
    …thinking not of society norms
      as he spoke to the shunned woman at the well;
    …ignoring community standing
      to stay with Zacchaeus, the tax collector;
    …setting aside pious cleanliness rules to reside with Simon the leper;
    …ignoring odors of body and clothing
      to enter the home of Simon the Tanner;
    …even daring to parody the oppressive presence of a foreign nation.

How indebted we are as well
  for inspiration from brothers and sisters in our own day,
    who from time to time show us how to hope, knowing not
      whether that hope will be realized in their own lifetime;
    who labor ceaselessly to eliminate injustices,
      though they themselves risk becoming a victim;
    who somehow persevere in a kind of forgiveness
      quite beyond the understanding of an untransformed heart.

So may we now turn with new resolve to the stones of our own walls,
  …breaking them down like these who have gone before;
    taking our place among those who continue to bring light
      to this Via de Cristo, …this Way of Christ.   – Amen

Widening the Circle

As we follow in the way of this Jesus,
    it's hard not to notice an ever-present pattern of widening circles.

Like the expanding ripples on a pond,
    Jesus' movements take him outside his circle of friends,
        beyond the boundaries of social convention,
            ...even those of his own religious tradition.

Gracious God,
    ...we are inclined to draw our circles just large enough
        to meet our needs,
            ...yet small enough for comfort.
But this life of Jesus seems to work differently.

Perhaps if we felt more keenly –
    ...feeling even as our own
        the pain of the outcast, lonely, and frightened,
            ...we might find our own circles growing larger.

Perhaps if we saw ourselves...
    Perhaps if every single one of us saw ourselves,
        as a unique and indispensable moving part
            in the Via de Cristo that is yet to be,
                ...we might find ourselves drawn into widening circles
            of awareness and adventure.

If we could but grasp that the presence of Jesus in our world
    is not only somehow resident within us,
        ...but *is* us,
            ...we might feel more strongly
                the True North of the compass within us,
            ...test more of our definitions of friendship,
            ...question more of the boundaries of social convention,
                ...and of our own religious traditions.

So may we, ...in time,
    ...find in ourselves that Jesus-like reordering of priorities,
        ...that widening of our own circles in the waters just ahead of us,
            ...in the Via de Cristo.   – Amen

Giving

Today, we turn our thoughts to giving,
  ...a way in which we mirror something
    of the Generous and Creative One, the very giver of life and being.
And though ours is a day of commitment that centers about our substance,
  it is also about celebration, ...and a milestone,
    ...another meaningful marker
      in the life of the fellowship we call Via de Cristo.

Gracious God,
  ...in our actions today, we acknowledge with gratitude
    those who began the work named Via de Cristo,
  ...those who planted, those who watered,
  ...those who nurtured when it was so young
    and full of uncertainties.

In our actions today we affirm their vision
  of a place of teaching and worship and praise
    that honors the invitation of the Christ
      through doors open in welcome to all;
  ...of a place where doubts and questions may be freely voiced;
  ...and of a people of faith who carry the compassion
    and loving-kindness of Christ into our community
      through service and advocacy and redemption.

In our actions today, we say to each other as a people,
  that together we are the ones who now take up this work so well begun,
    ...knowing it is still very much a work in progress.

Toward that end, may we give as we are able,
  generously, ...as a people blessed,
    and deeply as a people of vision.

And may we give because it was a taste of just such a vision
  that first drew us together
    into this remarkable expression of the Via de Cristo.   – Amen

Widow's Mite

With our eyes closed, we can almost see her,
...a woman in the shadows of the temple,
the worn folds and faded colors of her clothing her camouflage.

Nearly invisible, she waits,
...and in a moment when others step away,
she moves quickly to the alms-box.
Pausing only briefly,
her eyes closed and her lips moving in blessing,
she releases two small coins
that fall almost soundlessly into the box.
...And then she slips away,
...once more invisible among those gathered at the temple.

Gracious God,
...this story of the widow's mite is familiar to us,
...and its lessons timeless.

She has given the smallest of coins, ...yet no small gift at all;
...offered as if her two small coins mattered,
which they did,
...though less the coins themselves,
than her choice to reserve nothing, even in her own need.

Do not we encounter her footprints here along the Via de Cristo?

May we follow this widow's humble example.

May our offerings be measured by others' needs,
...and not what we have to offer.

And may our giving not be set casually adrift,
but sent on a course steered by our blessing,
and carried by the breath of our gratitude.   – Amen

Rest

How we treasure those rare moments
    when we can allow the subtle sounds of the forest
        to envelope us with their hushed presence,
            ...or invite the ocean waves to drown out all sounds
            save their own primal rhythms.

In this moment, we are no longer the conductor,
    directing the themes and harmonies of our lives;
        ...no longer the choreographer,
            ensuring that everyone about us
                observes their proper places and movements.

In this moment, we are the listener,
    ...eyes closed,
        ...surrendered,
            ...yet fully awake to the beauty of the moment.

We are inclined to think of these times as memorable treats.
    But the wisdom of Scripture deems them necessities,
        and names them Sabbath,
            ...full stops in each week for rest,
                ...for respite and recovery,
                    ...for reflection and dreaming,
                        ...for appreciation and gratitude,
                        ...and for listening;

            ...perhaps to hear the sounds of a sunrise,
                ...or just maybe to hear more clearly,
                that still small voice
                    that speaks to us from within.   – Amen

Humility (Personal Perspective)

This word – humility – is not a stranger to us in church life.
We recognize it as central to the teachings of Jesus,
...in both word and example.

And we see its expressions here and there,
...around and among us,
...one person quietly setting aside something of themselves
in order to benefit another,
...with neither expectation nor desire
of drawing attention or benefit of their own.

But is it yet a *way of life* among us?

Surely we are still learning how to "walk humbly with God,"
as in the words of the prophet Micah[9].

Gracious God,
there remains so much more to know of this humility
that we see everywhere in the teachings and life of Jesus.

In the days to come, may we discover more of its quiet,
but freeing and transforming power;
...opening ourselves to the pain and sorrow of others,
releasing a flow of compassion
...recognizing and freeing the latent possibilities in others;
...treasuring attention, recognition, and approval less;
...accepting more inconvenience and risk;

...finding ourselves following more closely the footsteps of this Jesus,
...in the Via de Cristo.   – Amen

Humility (Cosmic Perspective)

How curious that – like Alice in Wonderland –
  we human-creatures seem to be growing smaller and smaller.

The stars no longer inhabit a crystal dome above our heads,
  with the realm of God just beyond.

The Sun no longer circles about ourselves and our Earth;
  ...our Sun now just one of 100 billion neighbor stars;
    ...more distant neighbors yet of another half billion Milky Ways.

Once we were the unique and crowning glory
  of six days of God's creative work.
    Now we find ourselves a single expression
      of Creation's ongoing travail,
        ...just one tiny emergent speck
          in a stunningly immense cosmic landscape.

But still, we *are* here,
  ....remarkably and at the pleasure of the Ground of All Being;
    ...here, an expression of a Creation so elegantly imagined
      that it conceives within itself – layer upon layer –
        new creative things, ...in time including ourselves.

Though infinitesimally small in the cosmos, we are here, ...living,
  ...wonderfully complex, ...self-aware, social, ...curious and creative,
    ...and discovering new humility in our place in Creation,
      ...discovering new humility as well in our sense of Divine;
        ...drawn to a message of loving without reservation,
          ...serving without entitlement,
            ...giving without gain.

Divine Presence,
  though we have not yet learned humility well enough
    to discern your imprint in all we encounter;
      ...to quiet the hostilities among our kind;
        ...or even to lovingly safeguard our Earth-home,
  ...yet we are awakening to a new sense of your presence,
    ...and of your providence, and your trust in us;
  ...awakening to the growing weight in our unsteady, unready hands,
  ...awakening to a new way of understanding the words,
    "the meek shall inherit the Earth."[10] – Amen

Behind the Mask

How routinely we change roles as we move through life.
    Sometimes of necessity, sometimes by choice,
        we constantly make adjustments to our presence at work,
            at church, at home, in the business place,
        …changing shape and color in response to every demand
            that pulls us one way or another.

Something within ourselves may even worry,
    "If people really knew the real us …"

And so should we not pause from time to time,
    to set these demands aside for a moment to recall who we are?
        …making sure we have lost nothing of ourselves,
        …giving ourselves freedom and encouragement to explore
            every hint of latent promise
                present in the unfolding of our lives?

Holy Presence,
    we would be mindful that we are here at the impetus of the Divine.

Though we know so little, we sense that we are somehow
    part of the tangible expression of divine hope and intent,
        realized within the exquisite movements of Creation.

We would be mindful that we are created for each other,
    …else why crave one another's company?
    Why communication, cooperation, and laughter?
    Why teaching and learning? Why legacy? …Why love?

We would be mindful that we are created for the children brought to us;
    …a gift to us, …and in whom we see our future.

We would be mindful that in our uniqueness and diversity,
    we are each a product of divine vision;
        …each a new branch on an ever-spreading tree;
            …yet needing each other in a new way,
                each a loss if pruned or stunted.

Though our lives ebb and flow,
    may this essence of who we are remain undiminished,
        …basking in the glow of divine hope, …constant in gratitude,
        …faithful in stewardship of all you have placed in our charge,
            …including our essential selves.   – Amen

Dry Bones

Many of us have known the experience of Ezekiel's dry bones.

In the very places that first gave us spiritual life,
    we have found the spiritual part of us stalled,
        ...even wilting in well-intentioned simplicity and conformity,
          ...withering in places disappointingly devoid
            of questions and skepticisms and discovery.

But there are springs of sweet water, even in the deserts.

Gracious God,
    may this gathering always be a place of refuge and shelter,
        ...offering all the time in the world to heal
          from disappointment and hurt.

May we always be a place of restoration and renewal,
    ...where the inner joys of discovery and meaning can be learned,
        ...and regained.

May we always nurture curiosity and reflection,
    ...learning from each other,
        ...especially from the deepest of our questions and uncertainties.

And may we live in constant mindfulness that this is how we are created,
    ...in the benevolent providence that brings us to this place and time,
        ...and in this way
          in which we are in community with one another.   – Amen

Scripture - 1

We come to Scripture in so many different ways.
>Most of us are hearers of Scripture in worship services.
>>Some choose to read in the seclusion of special quiet spaces.

Some intentionally read Scripture in the unlikeliest of places
>because they find that it speaks with a different voice
>>in a subway or marketplace.

Though time and circumstance may change what we hear,
>the voice of Scripture always speaks to us in invitation,
>>…inviting us into awareness of the sacred,
>>>…and presence of the Divine,
>>…into history and tradition,
>>>…into questioning and change,
>>>>…into wisdom and humility,
>>>>>…into blessing, and being blessed,
>>>>>>…into an ever-deepening understanding of love.

Holy Presence,
>may the limitations of printed word and language never separate us
>from the essence of Scripture.

As we read, and reread these words,
>may their timeless, yet ever-evolving invitations draw us unerringly
>>toward lives full of grace and peace and healing
>>>…wherever our ways may take us.   – Amen

Scripture - 2

This morning we reflect on how Scripture,
   …ancient, yet revered,
     …can speak to us today
      in a world of science and independent thought.

Though distanced by a hundred generations and more from its writers,
   yet we have in common a sense of One Beyond Imagination
     whose Creation has brought into being all that we are,
      …and all that we yet might be.

And we share too that certain persistent hunger among our kind
   for ways to acknowledge and somehow relate to that reality.

A well of wisdom and insights; never old, never new,
   …it provokes us into conversation,
     …draws us into community.

A refuge, with words familiar and comforting,
   its ancient words still serve us in occasion and ceremony,
     …giving us continuity,
      …and tradition,
       …and so much more.

May Scripture always be to us what it has so benevolently been in the past,
   …a window,
    …or a well,
     …whatever it needs to be,
      …its words forever inadequate for their task,
       …waiting to take root,
        and grow, and blossom within us.   – Amen

Words

We turn our thoughts in these next few moments to our words,
 a part of our presence so familiar, and so taken for granted,
  that we might not otherwise take time to reflect on them,
   …even to consider them
    as a part of our giftedness and stewardship.

And yet, while they have no physical substance of their own,
 surely nothing else in our human experience
  is possessed of greater and everpresent consequence
   than our words.

Whether conveyed by sound or signs,
 our words are a hallmark of humanity.
But as we think together today,
 perhaps they are also a measure of our ability
  to allow others to see the Image of God imprinted within us.

Holy Presence,
 may then our words to community, and to our world,
  be those of peace and conciliation,
   …of welcome and affirmation,
    …of advocacy and inspiration.

May our words to those in our care foster love and confidence,
 …awareness and curiosity,
  …insight and compassion.

And may our words to ourselves be patient, encouraging, restorative,
 …and forgiving when needed.

May we grow in our ability to consider every utterance a creative moment,
 …for who among us can discern which of our words
  ultimately carry the potential for powerful
   and life-altering consequence.   – Amen

Small Violences

A prophetic voice from the near past asks,
  "*How can we live in the midst of a world
  marked by fear, hatred and violence,
  and not be destroyed by it?*"[11]

As if in response, we seem to hear the voice of Jesus echoing,
  "How can we live in the midst of this,
    ...and not do something about it?"

In countries not our own, ...in cities not our own,
  ...in neighborhoods not our own,
    ...the ferocity and pain of violence raises the defenses of our minds,
      ...and exceed our willingness,
        ...even our capacity to fully absorb them.

Yet, we choose to respond,
  ...seeking humanity and justice in community,
    and through our institutions of stewardship and faith.

But the essence of violence is harm,
  ...and the capacity to harm knows neither magnitude nor boundary,
    ...reaching even into the nearness of fellowships and families,
      ...and all too often, unrecognized.

Divine Presence,
  We would be mindful that even seemingly small things can harm;
    a raised voice, or a subtle drumbeat of criticism.

Even deferred conversations about important things
  can be unintended instruments of harm,
    ...to confidence and self-image, ...to imagination and adventure,
    ...to growth and opportunity, ...to relationships,
  ...perhaps harming even a sense of the future in our young,
    ...in whose hands rest the fate of generations yet to come.

May our paths lead to greater awareness in doing no harm,
  ...to initiative in undoing harm,
  ...to courage in preventing harm,
    ...for these contra-violent ways are surely a part
      of the Via de Cristo, ...the way of Christ.   – Amen

Imperfect Vessels

Today we think together about God's inclination
to accomplish extraordinary works through flawed people,
...in Scripture's words, entrusting treasure to earthen vessels.

We might ask, "What choice does God have,
given the imperfections of all humankind?"

Still, don't we carefully choose a rustic vase for wildflowers
precisely because its rough character complements
and shows off their beauty?

It's an idea both flattering and humbling,
...but might we have something in common with that rustic vase?

If we do what we are made to do,
are we not bearers of the beauty of God's love for all Creation?

If we do what we are asked to do,
do we not show off the beauty of God's love for all Creation?

If integrity and grace adorn our ways, flaws and all,
do we not complement the spectacular beauty of God's love
for every aspect of Creation?

Gracious God,
how intriguing it is that the goodness of your creation
allows imperfection to flow into beauty,
...and error to feed serendipity and even wisdom.

Because we don't always know how these fit together,
may we acknowledge our limitations and imperfections,
...but not allow them to hinder or slow our ventures
into unexplored territories of faith and action.   – Amen

Imperfect

This morning, we put aside for the moment the cloud of "shoulds"
and the "oughts" that surround us,
...those familiar words that suggest we have fallen short
of someone's idea – maybe even our own –
of what is truly good.

Instead, we pause to consider the still point of our faith,
...that "Nothing can separate us from the love of God."

Gracious God, in the freedoms that you have given us,
we find that we simply cannot live perfectly,
...cannot raise our children, ...or age perfectly,
...and cannot love perfectly.

And yet, here before us...
here all around us,
is the whole of sacred Creation;
...boundless and bountiful, ...and good,
...yea, very good.

And here we are, a part of that good Creation;
...with the very intent and hope of Creation somehow residing in us.

Still, we are works in progress,
never quite complete,
...and so we are never perfect,
but always learning,
...here in the goodness of Creation.

Spirit Among Us,
we love our children, even with their missteps.
And so we can believe that your love for us
is not diminished by our own stumblings.

May it be, then, that we are ever drawn toward the perfection
of that kind of love in all our walks of life,
...undeterred by our own imperfections.   – Amen

Grace

Imagine for a moment what the world would be like without grace;
...a relentless place of sharp edges,
of escalating anger and eye-for-an-eye justice;
a place without peacemakers, or forgiveness,
...or second chances;
...a place with no one to walk hand in hand with us
when overwhelmed by rage, or worry, or grief.

In its quiet power, grace reaches beyond anger, hurt, and indignation;
...even beyond our own failures.
Given freely, it draws on something greater than ourselves;
...on something within us we have come to know
through the one called Jesus,
...who calls us to seek healing beyond hurt,
...and redemption beyond failure,
...even when the failures are our own.

These are the beloved words of poet Annie Flint,[12]

He giveth more grace when the burdens grow greater,
He sendeth more strength when the labors increase,
To added affliction He addeth His mercy,
To multiplied trials, His multiplied peace.
...His love has no limit, His grace has no measure,
...He giveth and giveth and giveth again.

Whether a moment of grace will change only the moment,
...or a lifetime,
...we cannot know.

But grace may be the most important thing we can know,
...because we can offer grace,
even in places where we don't yet know how to love.   – Amen

Grace in Flight

The beauty of migrating geese in flight belies their strength;
　　the feather-light movement of the dancer
　　　　gives no hint of her devotion to practice.
　　　　　　It is their grace that looses them from earth's captive hold,
　　　　　　　....and they are free to fly.

There is a certain kinship here
　　with the grace spoken of in our sacred writings;
　　　　...where strengths born of practice
　　　　　　are also prelude to flight and freedom.

As in the ballet, and the flight of the geese,
　　this grace of Scripture is not a solitary endeavor,
　　　　but one that draws us uniquely into one another's lives;
　　　　　　in ways still new to us,
　　　　　　　　...but reverberating in the call of this one called Jesus.

So Gracious God,
　　when the powerful but sightless quakes and storms of our island-world
　　　　bring pain and loss and misery to our brothers and sisters,
　　　　　　...may we fly to their aid, bringing strength to their weakness,
　　　　　　and healing to their wounds.

As followers of Jesus,
　　may we become a voice among the silent,
　　　　a presence among the invisible,
　　　　　　an advocate among the helpless and marginalized,
　　　　　　　　and hope for the oppressed everywhere about us.

And in our own day-to-day walks in family and community,
　　may we become well-practiced in setting aside anger and indignation,
　　　　...in overlooking and forgiving,
　　　　　　...in restoring and encouraging.

In such ways, may we grow as faithful emissaries of this wondrous grace
　　that frees from the gravities of the world,
　　　　...everywhere our lives take us
　　　　　　...in the Via de Cristo.　– Amen

Barnabas

Holy Presence,
    who is a Barnabas in our life?

Who is that unique one who works
    in openness and trust alongside us,
        – with words, or without –
           …to quietly help us accomplish our work
               better than we might by ourselves?

May we recognize the Barnabas in the quietness of his or her ways,
    whether a sustaining presence in our lives, or perhaps a fleeting one;
        the Barnabas who seeks only to help,
           coming alongside us without need of visibility or fanfare.

May we recognize when to seek out a Barnabas in our own circumstance,
    …making the difference between good and best in our work.

And may we honor the Barnabas gift
    by freely becoming a Barnabas as well when the opportunity invites us,
        …for that too is a part of this Via de Cristo,
           …as we understand it,
              …and seek to practice it.   – Amen

Reality Check

It's not the easy times that test what we are made of,
but the difficult ones.

And so it is, that in that moment when we walk away from a situation
with anger, or with hurt,
...the measure begins to be taken
of how well we have taken to heart
the example and teachings of Jesus.

Gracious God, when we are hurt by others,
may we be reserve room for grace to turn the hurt into healing.

Should we be provoked to anger,
may we listen carefully, and practice restraint,
...always leaving room for reconciliation.

And when we react in judgment,
...as we so quickly and easily do,
...may we recall – even in that moment –
...that we are quickest to find shortcomings
that we are most familiar with,
...those that reflect our own.

Spirit of Unity,
we know these encounters are human,
...and real,
...but we also know your constant call
to works of mercy, and grace, and healing.

So may we seek,
...and practice this better way
until it lives within us.   – Amen

Privilege

When we hear the words, "People of Privilege,"
    we might envision people with lands and titles,
        and households of persons of lower status, ...in servitude,
            looking after the comfort and well-being of the privileged.

The distance maintained between those served, and those in service,
    strikes us as quaint, and a thing of the past.

But are we not – with our own wealth and distances -
    more like these "People of Privilege" than we might like to think?

Gracious God,
    we have chosen the name, and the way of Christ,
        ...a path in which we strive to infuse privilege with gratitude,
            sharing generously and selflessly of the gifts of life,
                and of the bounty of Creation itself,
                    ...closing the distances separating us from our kin.

So in this time of worldwide madness and bloodshed,
    may we find courage to take one step beyond powerlessness,
        ...as peacemakers in our own life-space.

In this time of sweeping natural and man-made disaster,
    ...may we find compassion to weep with them,
        ...and then take one step beyond the limits of comfort,
            ...toward rescue and restoration.

As poverty and injustice seems to continue unabated,
    ...may we find determination to take one step past our own boundaries,
        ...to extend the limits of redemption.

Giver of All That Blesses Us,
    ...whether our steps be large or small,
        may we grow in conviction
            that true privilege lies in opportunity to weigh in conscience
                the distances between ourselves and those in greater need;
            ...growing as well in the ability and will
                to respond in service and selflessness
                    to close those distances.   – Amen

Precious in His Eyes

Our faith understanding tells us that love somehow spans
    the unthinkable abyss between humankind and Creator;
        …telling us that this Jesus,
           who is the translator of this kind of love for us,
             says simply that we are all, …all,
                …precious in the eyes of the Creator.

And yet, we are inclined to draw our own circles small,
    keeping outside those circles even others of our own kind
        who are somehow a little different from us,
           …pushing them out of sight,
           …out of mind.

But in a reflective moment, we doubt whether the creator of life itself
    measures anything in terms of wealth, clothing, color,
        language, orientation, or even shape or ability.

Gracious God,
    may we learn to better see the homeless, the immigrant,
        and the less able through Jesus' eyes
           as our own lives intersect theirs,
           …to recognize them as one of your own,
               …seeing them in the light of promise, not prejudice.

And may we learn to reach still further,
      …beyond our stereotypes and boundaries,
        …to bring a touch of mercy, and justice,
           and restoration, and presence,
               to those who experience so little of them.
               For these are surely the workings of real love.

May we learn to practice them with more consistent and constant grace,
    …until we learn to love;
      …until we see with new eyes;
        …until these, our brothers and sisters,
          become precious in our eyes,
            even as they are in yours.   – Amen

Loving Ourselves

We have been told, ...by some in times past,
   ...and by others in our own time, that we are created spiritual outcasts,
      rogues and wretches that rebel against God,
         ...wounded and broken,
            ...deserving nothing of the grace of God.

But a very different message persists
   through the words and life of this one called Jesus,
      ...a message of a transcendent love that trumps every shortcoming.

And the voice of Creation itself echoes that we have each been entrusted
   – as individuals, and as a people –
      with a precious portion of this unfathomable universe.

Though we humans are in many ways kindred in kind,
   the wondrous workings of this universe curiously require
      that no two of us are exactly alike,
         ...each of us unique among all the infinities of time and space,
            ...no one else thinking as we do, seeing and hearing as we do,
               able to do exactly what we do.

Holy Presence, in a moment like this,
   we recognize that we cannot know the importance of being who we are.

So may we summon new courage to explore ourselves,
   alert for the greater opportunities that arise,
      even while refining our sensitivity to the smaller ones,
         ...knowing not which might open
            a whole new realm of possibility,
               ...perhaps even redeeming life itself.

Gracious God, we also find it easy to be held back
   by certain mistakes we have made,
      laboring under burdens created by a younger, less aware,
         perhaps more foolish version of ourselves.
   So may we learn the lightening of love and forgiveness,
      ...even of ourselves.

And may we be ever watchful for that unexpected someone else
   who just may reshape a piece of the puzzle that we are;
      or with whom we just might accomplish the yet-unimagined,
         as we continue exploring together in this Via de Cristo.   - Amen

Compassion

We who have gathered together here this morning
    have named ourselves as followers of the one named Jesus.

As we search our sacred writings, a constant flow of compassion
    is revealed through his life and teachings.

We have some of that same gift within us,
    perhaps a reflection of the one who gave us life and being.

We can sometimes feel a measure of the hurt or desperation
    experienced by another,
        …and the most desperate or compelling circumstance
          moves us on occasion to reach deeply in response.

And yet, the numbing magnitude and ever-presence of human need
    and pain in our world, …and the skepticism we have learned,
        …and the busyness of our day-to-day routines
          surely dim our vision and dull our senses
            to human need in the everyday.

Still, Gracious God,
    something within us suggests that the freedom we give this single gift
        – the gift of empathy and compassion –
          may be a true measure of our discipleship.

So may we test ourselves, asking whether today is a day of compassion.
    May our indifferences give way to awakening.
        May we allow ourselves to feel more keenly
          the hungers and pains of others we encounter.

May we learn to act immediately, freely, and selflessly,
    simply because we can;
        …because in all of Creation,
          we have been most blessed with the capacity for compassion.

May skepticism, and irritation, and inconvenience give way
    to possibilities of healing, recovery, reconciliation,
        …perhaps even redemption to new life.

And may we come to know deep within that our every act of compassion,
    …whether large or small, …whether known to others or not,
        …changes things, …even if only ourselves.   – Amen

Forgiveness

This way of Jesus seems to be simple in the hearing,
 but not so easy in practice.
Just follow me – Jesus says – until you *also* learn The Way.
 But then he uses troubling words like, "forgive."

It's a meddlesome and nosey word, this "forgive,"
 with its way of shining light
  into the more hardened and broken places in our hearts.
Plainspoken from the cross, it unmasks our self-centeredness,
 …and reveals our arbitrariness and inconsistencies.

It's an impatient word, this "forgive."
 We want it to be an every-now-and-then kind of thing,
  …when the circumstances are right …for us.
 Still, …we find ourselves praying,
  "*Forgive us our trespasses, as we forgive those who trespass against us,*"
   …trying to learn some more difficult,
    everyday, all-the-time kind of forgiveness.

Divine Presence,
 we do not walk in The Way without stumbling.
  We probably never will.
   But may we never cease to feel your attraction
    toward a more peaceful and healing and redemptive
    way of being in our world.

May we have the courage to search out those offenses
 that we have harbored, …or caused.
May we confront every condition we have attached to forgiveness.
 Where we find a wound, may forgiveness bring healing.
  Where we find a flame, may forgiveness bring its quenching.

May forgiveness become a strong current
 in the living waters that flow through us,
  …waters that take little notice of a misstep,
   …like ripples from a thrown pebble.

May we – in time – come to recognize a simple truth,
 that where no offense is given,
  …*and no offense is taken,*
   …there is no need for forgiveness.   – Amen

Reconciliation

This thing we call trust seems like quicksilver in our world,
  so fluid and beautiful,
    and yet lost so easily in a single careless instant.

Parts of our world are aflame with the distrust of ancient hatreds.
  Our trusted institutions, …even families and friendships often fail us.
  We feel immersed in turbulent and constant ebbs and flows
    of broken faith, expectations, and boundaries.
    We struggle, and wish it were otherwise.

But Gracious God,
  as followers of this one called the Christ –
    we are recognizing that the Via de Cristo calls us into his work,
      …calls us even into the work of redeemer,
        …into the redemptive work of reconciliation.

So may it be that we have ears to hear when it's our own time,
  …even the hardest of times, when reconciliation gets very personal,
    …when we are called to make the first move,
      …when we believe we have been wronged.

May our eyes – if only briefly –
  be those of the Christ who sees only another child,
    …a child beloved of God.

May we reach deep inside ourselves
  to set aside ego, hurt, anger, pride, and history,
    – all that is of lesser, …even insignificant value –
      …and find the strength to offer our hand,
        or voice, or presence in reconciliation,
          …perhaps even for a second or third time.

And if rejected – for now –
  may we also find the resolve to leave the way open,
    …selflessly, …without condition,
      for that too is the Via de Cristo. – Amen

Loving My Enemy

This morning, Scripture reminds us once again
　　that love is the ultimate litmus test for all of what we do in life.

In some perfect world, we think,
　　perhaps we could somehow learn to love even our enemies
　　　　as much as we do ourselves.
But on an ordinary day,
　　looking at the strangers standing with us on an ordinary street corner,
　　　　it seems an impossibility.
We just don't seem to be able to feel that Jesus-kind of love.

Gracious God,
　　perhaps we have thought this Jesus-love should blossom in us
　　　　like the lovely thing we have known with those closest to us,
　　　　　　…kind and generous, …vulnerable without risk,
　　　　　　　　…a love that is so easy.

Yet the life of Jesus
　　– and the unflinching message of Scripture –
　　　　seems to show a relentless love that endures through harder stuff,
　　　　　　…occasionally at great personal expense.

Holy Presence,
　　though we may not feel that certain kind of affection
　　　　toward everyone in view,
　　　　　　may we grow in awareness of the greater love
　　　　　　　　that is in play among us.

May we then choose to pay greater attention to those around us,
　　… generous in time and substance.
May we be moved to confront error and injustice,
　　…with courage, and kindness, and compassion.
May we engage in difficult conversation, determined to take no offense.
May we foster forgiveness, and reconciliation,
　　…and find ways to redeem those who have somehow lost their way.
May we uplift always, …and be patient in all we do.

Love does these things. …Jesus-love does these things.
　　And should we dare to offer these even to our enemies,
　　　　perhaps they too will in time recognize it as love,
　　　　　　…learned from the Christ,
　　　　　　　　…and offered to them along the Via de Cristo.　 - Amen

One Step Toward Shalom

Shalom is a gift word to us,
    an ancient word from halfway around the world.
        Sometimes a greeting, sometimes a word of parting,
            …it is always an invocation of God's blessing,
                …a blessing framed in the larger hope
                    and anticipation of God's Shalom,
                        …when all of Creation finds its way to peace
                        and reconciliation.
Gracious God,
    in this moment – even as we acknowledge your presence –
    we are slow to see how some of our own actions
        stand in the way of your Shalom.

So on this day of celebrating relationships,
    …where there is silence born of an accidental wound,
    an unguarded word, or a misunderstanding,
        …whether it be our silence, or another's,
            …may we take one step toward breaching the silence,
            …and toward your Shalom.

Where there is distance born of broken trust, or promise, or expectation,
    …whether it be our distance, or another's,
        may we take one step toward reconciliation,
            …and toward your Shalom.

Where there are barriers of pride, or risk of failure,
    or just not knowing what to do or say,
        …may we reach beyond them,
            transforming belief into acts of faith,
                …and movement toward your Shalom.

Even as we extend the hand of Christ's peace to each other today,
    may your grace and peace stir our hearts to take that next difficult step,
        …toward restoration of a troubled relationship,
            …and toward your Shalom. – Amen

Bridges (Intercession)

Our prayers on behalf of one another build sacred bridges
   between need and divine providence,
      ...spanning abysses of pain and loss,
        ...narrowing the breach between plight and possibility,
         ...and making a way where there seems to be none.

Gracious God,
   our war-weary world is in deep need.
Teach us – brothers and sisters of all peoples – to pray always
   for seemingly distant peace among the nations,
     ... for healing of the afflicted, recovery from disaster,
     restoration of the displaced,
       ...and sustenance for those who perish in privation.

Our nation drifts in deep need.
Teach us – who share one flag – to pray always for those who govern,
   ...for those who deal with the aftermath of violent pasts,
     ...whose vision has given way to nearsighted contention.
May their actions return to wisdom, principle, courage, and justice.

Our city struggles in deep need.
Teach us to pray daily for those thrown into financial tumult,
   ...for the hungry and homeless,
     ...for those whose chosen work is respite and recovery,
       ...and for those whose enterprises will in time
       bring financial relief to those without work.

Brothers and sisters in fellowship are experiencing deep need.
Teach us each to pray for these within arm's reach.
   May we *become* that sacred bridge,
     ...through advocacy, assistance, and assurance,
       ...lending a consoling hand, a comforting arm,
         ...a shoulder or an ear,
           ...or perhaps just our presence.
            May we become the prayer.   – Amen

Millions of words – in a hundred languages –
  describe how desperately we need one another,
    and in so many different ways.
And still we are inclined to devalue and distance each other
  with such seeming ease.

Today, we focus on a single helpful word, ..."Ubuntu,"
  ...a sophisticated word we borrow from a tribal people an ocean away,
    ...a word that echoes a message quite familiar.

Spirit Among Us,
  this is a lovely soft heartbeat of a word, ..."Ubuntu,"
    ...calling us to a way of living that is aware of the connectedness,
      and interdependence, and value of all of humankind,
    ...calling us to set aside the myriad ways we have devised
      to estrange and segregate ourselves.

Ubuntu invites us into availability and affirmation,
  into selfless works of compassion and justice;
    invites us into dignity, ...and the security of community,
      ...and so much more.

The Via de Cristo and Ubuntu are of like fabric,
  ...enfolding us in a profound sense of oneness,
    ...then reaching still further with respect and reconciliation
      to welcome those who are strangers and alien to us,
        ...inviting us as well to rediscover them as friends and kin
          in this single household of the Creator.

Spirit Within Us, may Ubuntu become a practice made perfect in us
  ...as we walk with one another
    in the way of the one called Jesus.   – Amen

Ubuntu - 2/4

We speak today of oneness,
   the substance of Jesus' parting prayer for his disciples,
      and for followers throughout time.

Was this prayer for oneness a prayer unanswered?
   Or was this benediction one last loving affirmation
      of a higher way of living in a very real world
         filled with imperfect and sometimes challenging people?

Holy Presence,
   may we walk in abiding awareness of our calling into oneness.

May we do well the easier things of oneness,
   …of mutual caring, and respect, and harmony.

But may we also faithfully practice the sometimes harder things,
   like the graceful accommodation of differences
      among us that provoke us,
         …sometimes to thought,
            sometimes to passion,
               …and sometimes, over time, even to change.

And may our message, and our example,
      be calls to a oneness that is profoundly boundary free,
         …knowing nothing of color, class, or creed,
         …knowing nothing of organizations, nations, or geography,
         …knowing only the boundless love
            crafted into the whole of Creation.   – Amen

What an extraordinary time we live in,
    …blessed by imagination, curiosity, creativity, vision,
        and passion as never before.
    Future-altering change has become almost commonplace,
        even expected.

In our hands, we can hold the means for instantly connecting
    to kindred souls oceans apart;
        …forming new communities and networks,
        …finding new ways to act in community more quickly
        and in larger numbers than ever before,
           …even reshaping the futures of nations.

Spirit Among Us,
    …may we continue to reflect Ubuntu, as far as we can reach,
      discovering and realizing the full potential for good
      in these new opportunities,
        …growing in community,
        …expanding our definition of community
          even as our own networks grow,
        …and more effectively advancing and sharing
          the spiritual dimensions of life
            with kindred spirits in the Via de Cristo,
            …the Way of Christ. – Amen

Ubuntu - 4/4

We have been thinking together about that certain need within us
　　to live in the richness of relationship;
　　　　…and a way of being that knows down deep
　　　　　　that we fully flourish as individuals only
　　　　　　　　when our lives are woven into community,
　　　　　　　　…when they are somehow entangled in a lovely way
　　　　　　　　　　in mutual benevolence and in need of one another,
　　　　　　　　…so that your laughter is mine, and your pain as well,
　　　　　　　　…so that I feel you even when you are far away.

This sounds so familiar.
　　Are we talking about Ubuntu,
　　　　…or about the way of Jesus?
　　　　　　Are they two streams that converge?
　　　　　　Or are they but a single stream?

Gracious God,
　　surely we are speaking of a wisdom and a way
　　　　that transcends language, and history,
　　　　　　and the boundaries we draw for ourselves,
　　　　　　…a way that perhaps even touches the sacred,
　　　　　　　　…that touches the hope you have in us
　　　　　　　　　　and for our place in your Creation.

May it be that we are drawn ever toward a sense of greater community,
　　…toward humility and generosity,
　　　　…toward blessing and being blessed.

May our way be marked by kindness and compassion,
　　and restoration and even adventure,
　　　　as we follow the path of Ubuntu, and the Way of Christ.　– Amen

Being Salt - 1

In many cultures around the world, guests are made welcome
  with a gift of a small loaf of bread and small vessel of salt;
    ...the bread to satisfy a traveler's hunger;
      the precious salt to please the guest's palate.

In this, ...our special day of welcoming,
  ...the bread we share carries additional meaning,
    ...and the Jesus tradition calls us to be salt.

Holy Presence, in the days to come, may we live in the simplicity of salt,
  ...with clarity and purpose in all we do.

May we live in the consistency of salt,
  ...preserving and enhancing everything we touch.

And may we live in the ubiquity of salt, ...
  ...being found anywhere and everywhere we might make a difference.

May we – like salt – change all that we touch for the better,
  ...and may we in turn be transformed as well,
    ...as the good news of Scripture comes to life in our hands,
      and in our hearts.   – Amen

Being Salt - 2

Today we speak of the gift of salt.
    The oceans are full of it;
        there would be no life without it.
            Yet, no life exists where it is present in excess.

We have warred over it, used it in religious observances,
    and used it to seal covenants and friendships.

We have given it in hospitality, used it for money,
    and used it to disinfect and preserve.

But always and ever, we have used it to make our food taste better.

Scripture speaks often of salt to suggest how we should be
    as we make our way among those who share Creation with us,
        …that our way be marked by the nuancing
            and enhancing of the flavors of life,
                …of others, and of those among us.

In this way, Scripture says our paths in life should be of significance,
    full of meaning and intellect and adventure,
        …complemented by grace and compassion,
            …lest lives, and life itself, be left bland and tasteless
            in our absence.

So may we learn this way of being salt in our world,
    of seasoning our relationships,
        …of spicing our conversations with meaning
            and possibility and compassion,
                so that by ones or twos, …or in community,
                    the full potential of Creation may be realized in us,
                        …and in the world we are blessing in your name. – Amen

Leavening

How many of our sacred Scriptures speak of works of great consequence
  beginning in the hand or voice of one
    who has little standing among mankind?

Creation itself has revealed that we cannot know with certainty
  whether even the smallest happening is ultimately of importance or not,
    telling us that we are all connected,
      and dependent upon each other in ways
        that stretch far beyond even our imagination.

And so it is that sacred scripture calls us to respond because we can,
  ...when we find need, ...where we find distress,
    simply because we are brothers and sisters,
      and fellow travelers in this divine Creation.

Holy Presence, ...how slow we seem to be to hear
  what the agreement of these voices is saying to us.

Our common prayer through the centuries has been
  that your kingdom come into being on earth,
    imagining that you would – in the fullness of time –
      somehow bring that about.

But we are finally recognizing that this mission of peace and of restoration
  is to take shape in our own hands, else why our peculiar ability
    to dream and create, to cooperate,
      and to make choices that give shape to,
        ...even *redirect* our futures?

May we learn to live in greater optimism and hope,
  in greater presence and empathy, in greater awareness that we know not
    the ultimate consequence of even the smallest act of kindness,
      or word of inspiration or restoration.

May we be in our world even as the leaven in the baker's bread,
  living and spread throughout,
    reaching its full potential as it reshapes and redefines
      a formless flour-dusted lump in readiness
        for its transformation into a life-sustaining loaf
        for all who would partake.

May we be no less than that in our world.   – Amen

Encounters

Constant in all of Creation is that when two of its parts,
  ...whether large or small, ...encounter one another,
    ...in even the slightest of ways, ...both are changed.
Atoms may find only directions or speeds changed.
But nebulas, among the enormities of the heavens,
    ever so slowly swallow one another,
      merging into a single greater one of its kind;
        ...atoms and star clusters alike, moving, encountering,
          guided only by four simple laws of nature.

Holy Presence, the greater mystery
  is that in our own peculiar middle place
    among these greatest and smallest of Creation,
      we are almost unaware of such rules,
        ...our physical beings only occasionally
          noticeably changed
            by encounters with one another.

Yet in some entirely new way,
  something within us is surely changed by such encounters.
    Though often differing in degree, we are changed,
      ...both of us.

In this Via de Cristo we are asked to stop,
  and look at all of our brothers and sisters in a new way,
    recognizing in each moment of encounter
      that we are a treasure held in each others' hands.

We have learned that we cannot know
  the ultimate importance of even the smallest act.
    ...We cannot know how the script of either of our lives
      may be changed by a touch, a meeting of eyes,
        the exchange of a word or two,
          a shared experience or insight,
            or simply the making of new acquaintance.

So, gracious God, however fleeting or enduring our encounters,
  may our choices, our actions, and our words in the moment
    always seek to help rather than hurt, build rather than erode,
      embellish rather than stain,
        ...always expressing the love that Jesus taught,
          ...fostering the greater good within both of us
            that awaits only our bidding.   – Amen

Ambassadors

We have been speaking in these recent days of love,
of the varied expressions of this Christ-emulating love,
...a love of the widest sweep,
reaching as far as the most marginalized and difficult,
...and as near as our own troubled and inconsistent selves.

And yet, on this day, all about us is a world aflame,
seemingly devoid of such compassion.

Whether half a world away, or only a few blocks,
this new ether drags their warrings and dyings
before our reluctant eyes.

...And somewhere in this life given to us,
we seem to unavoidably encounter that deeply troubling,
perhaps frightening circumstance,
when the light of this Christ-like love seems to dim,
...feeling simplistic,
...perhaps even suddenly irrelevant.

Holy Presence, may a sense grow...
May even our faith grow in us,
with knowledge that the strength of this Christ-kind love
quietly persists, even when our eyes are dimmed;
...and now we are its ambassador.

May we recognize that this particular path is our charge,
...this ground passing beneath our feet,
...this world passing within our reach.

May we find a greater consistency in being – moment to moment –
the living presence of this healing, peacemaking, forgiving,
affirming, and rebuilding kind of love
that we have come to know in the Via de Cristo,
...steadily pushing back against mankind's worst;
not a moment to lose; no opportunity to squander.

May our awareness be heightened, our compassion deepened.
May our resolve be strengthened, ...our rushes to judgment slowed.
May we be instant and constant in our wearing of this mantle,
...as ambassadors of this Christ-kind love,
this way of being that we are still learning
in the Via de Cristo.   – Amen

God-Kind Love

This morning we revisit the highest way of being to which we are called,
...reminded once again
that the entirety of the law and the prophets of Scripture
derives from just two admonitions,
to love God, and to love our neighbors as ourselves.

So simple in words, ...this calibration of our internal compass,
...this ultimate distillation of all that Scripture has to say
to guide us in our living;
...and yet seemingly so far out of human reach.

How can we do this impossible thing
when we feel such God-kind love toward so few in our own lives,
...let alone the multitudes
that lie well outside our many kinds of circles?

Holy Presence,
perhaps we err in taking the measure of our own love.
Perhaps we should be asking,
"What does your love look like to others? ...through us?"

Even now we hear a quiet echo of Scripture naming us servants
...and stewards, ...even ambassadors,
called to represent and express this boundary-less
God-kind love to all,
...but especially to those not yet drawn inside our circles.

So may we learn to regularly take even small tours of faith
outside the bounds of our perceived limitations,
...beyond our well-rehearsed and unconsciously practiced biases,
...loosening our grip on anger and resentments
that bind us still to some past circumstance,
...and the fears and uncertainties that slow our present pace
and dampen our anticipation,

...taking tours of faith that bring us as neighbors to others,
with unexpected expressions of kindness and restoration,
of compassion and healing and hope,
...expressions which may be indistinguishable from love;
but if not love,
then at least expressions of grace.   – Amen

In God's Image

How is it that we may somehow, …in some way,
   …be created in God's image?
     As one thing usually resembles another,
      we are not even sure how to think about this.

As creations, we recognize the Author of Creation
     as immensely "other" in its being,
      …infinitely greater yet than any human words or imaginings.

But creations themselves often speak to us of their creators,
   …of their ways, …of their intent, …of their vision.
And the breathtaking message on the very first page
   of our universe's Creation's story is that Creation is ordered,
     …and provident, …and discoverable.

Its invitation – graved in stars and stone –
   calls us to explore and ponder deeply about Creator
   …and Creation, …because we can.

Creative Presence,
   we have sometimes made too much,
     and sometimes too little of what and who we are in Creation.

We are surely gifted with a knowledge of both good and evil.
   Still – though we have the freedom to err –
     we also have the unique capacity to imagine,
      …to create, …to inspire,
   …to act in unselfish, even sacrificial benevolence,
   …to nurture and heal,
   …to change circumstance, even the direction
     and destiny of people's lives,
      …to create beauty, …and to love.
And we can accomplish even more and greater
   through our numbers and diversities,
     …through our mobilities and collaborations.

Are these, then, reflections of the divine in us?
   We can only guess.

Still, we can be constantly mindful of both our privilege and stewardship,
   …and not remain merely bystanders, lest we squander,
     even profane that which is divinely imprinted in us,
      and so remarkably entrusted into our hands. – Amen

SEASONS

Traditions

The rich traditions of our faith affect us in so very many ways,
  profoundly shaping our search for meaning
    and encounter with the Divine.

Spirit Among Us,
  let us continue to be mindful of our stories, symbols, and seasons,
    ...that connect us with our roots,
      and the insights of those who preceded us.

May our sacred art and music and writings
  continue to bless, teach, illuminate,
    ...and inspire us in thought and action.

May our observances, and our ceremonies
  continue to celebrate our passages and milestones,
    ...with their order and apparel
      setting aside these moments from the ordinary.

May we appreciate even the forms and appearances of our gathering places,
  whether marked by spires or simplicity,
    as they frame our sense of presence with the Divine.

May we continue to respect and honor the best of our traditions,
  even as we build new ones on cornerstones of the old.

May we be especially mindful of the essentials woven into them,
  ...as they order our priorities,
    ...and as we leave them as tradition
      for the generations to come.   – Amen

The hustle and bustle, and lights and sounds of Christmas
    are once again fading.
And we stand in a moment of quiet,
    on the threshold of yet another new year,
        …a moment that invites us to once again reflect
          on the substance of the year past,
            … as we begin setting our intentions and directions
              for the new year.

What of the year past shall we leave behind?
    And what shall we carry into the new, so that what we do
      – individually, and collectively as a people – truly matters?

And how shall we adjust the directions of our lives in this New Year
    to better reflect the heart of the faith walk we have chosen?

Gracious God,
    …may we find ways to bring more of ourselves, …and our passions,
      …into the situations and opportunities that confront us.

May we grow as family, in its many ways of being.

May we grow in visibility and vision as an attractive, venturesome,
    and restorative community of faith.

And may we be part of a greater voice in our world
    that will not be silenced in its calls for peace, and reason,
      and integrity, and justice.

May all that we do in the days to come
    nurture and encourage, …create and transform, heal and redeem,
      for that is what we understand to be our work
        in this New Year,
          …in this Via de Cristo,
            …this Way of Christ.   – Amen

New Year - 2

We have just stepped over the threshold.
 It's a new dawn, …a new day, …in a brand new year.

The successes, …and the shortfalls of the year past
 have brought us thus far.
  But now they lie behind us.

Ahead of us are all the unwritten pages of this New Year,
 …so full of potential and opportunity.

And how remarkably gifted we are,
 with abilities to transform these possibilities into fresh realities.

So let us greet opportunity with anticipation and optimism,
 …and let our passions light the way
  when the path grows faint or rough.

May we never tire of the adventure of encountering your presence,
 and of your way to live in the world.

May we persist in doing good in a world capable as well of darkness,
 …drawing on deep-rooted determination
  as we encounter adversity and discouragement.

May our successes be marked by generosity and humility,
 …as we seek new and meaningful ways
  to touch people and change lives.

And may our own presence be transformed in the process
 through love and grace found in the Via de Cristo. – Amen

This morning, as we stand in silent wonder,
    the sun rises into a new day, ...into a new year as we measure it.
Our eyes closed to the suddenness of its brilliance,
    we welcome the return of its life-giving warmth.

Immobilized in this moment, ...in this unique place
    between an unchangeable past, and a future yet to be written,
        we have momentarily laid aside the man-things
            that define and constrain,
                and deceive us into being less than what we truly are.

In the light of this sun, we are a new thing,
    a never-before-flowering of the immensely moving
        and creative mystery that is our universe;
    yet more than that, ...a mystery within a mystery,
        ...a miracle birth within a Creation that ignores unlikelihoods;
        ... born with our own remarkable infusion of creative capacities.

Holy Presence, in this moment of reflection,
    we are mindful that no other in our island world
        can imagine and dream like we can,
            ...invent and build, ...repair and restore.
None other can heal the ailing and bind up the wounded,
    ...can learn from the marginal and unconventional,
        ...benefit from our mistakes,
            ...and teach whole new generations yet to come.
None can love, ...or forgive, as we do at our best.

Still, ...we are mindful that we have capacities as well
    to inflict harm, quench hope, oppress,
        ...and take lives and destroy in a thousand new ways.

If only we could know the true value of this new day,
    ...as we begin penning the future into these now-blank pages.

Knowing instead only that it abounds with fresh new possibilities,
    may we – as we begin our new year's walk in the Via de Cristo –
        move more resolutely toward that peculiarly delicate balance point
        between privilege and stewardship,
        ...toward finding a way to somehow live in this world
            as both creative sovereign
                and compassionate servant. – Amen

First Sacred Book

This morning, in our first tentative steps into this new year,
  we pause for a moment to consider the interleavings
    of the pages of the two great books
      that have informed and shaped our lives in the journey so far,
        ...as they will continue to do in the days before us.

As a gathered people,
  we have always called ourselves people of the Bible,
    the book that collects the experience and understandings
      of many who from earlier centuries speak to us still
        of their own passionate searchings for understanding,
          and the will and presence of the Divine.

But the rustling pages of the earliest of all sacred writings
  also lie before us, open as never before;
    ...as Creation itself patiently continues to voice
      its own timeless story,
        ...remarkable and unchanging,
          ...ever-disclosing,
            ... unfettered by limits of language
              or human understanding.

Spirit among us, ...how blessed we are to live in a time
  in which these two books are free to speak to us
    in their own unique duet,
      teaching us as never before of both Creation and Author.

How grateful we must be as well for the remarkable gift of curiosity
  that draws us so strongly into such exploration and insight.
    May we do nothing to diminish its inviting call
      into the vast new realms beyond the knowing of the present.

May we honor the questioning of our certainties;
  may we teach always with an open mind;
    and may we never lose the awe and wonder
      of the who and how and what of ultimate beginnings,
        of the unfathomable miracle of all Creation,
          and of the miracle of finding ourselves
            in just such a place of promise,
              on the threshold of this new year.   – Amen

Martin Luther King Day

In our time together this morning,
    we are remembering one whose very name evokes the words,
        "I have a dream."
That vision – rooted in his faith – drew him to become a living catalyst,
    …raising our nation's conscience and resolve
        to act against racial injustice.

There is an unmistakable echo in his dying.
    …A man of peace, he nonetheless died in violence,
        leaving a work well-begun in the hands of those left behind,
        …and there is much yet to be done;

    …for it seems that human hatred and greed
        will always find ways to waste imagination and potential
           through warring and exploitation
               based on skin color, or histories, or faith,
                 …or other imagined offense.

Holy Presence,
    …how grateful we are for this resolute dreamer,
        …for those who dreamed with him,
        …for the measure of progress made in this country,
        …and for the reminder that this dream is but a part
           of the greater dream of Him whose name we have taken.

May we be ever vigilant for opportunities – whether large or small –
    to turn the vision of Jesus into action.

May we be open to the call should that dream beckon *us*,
    …for a season, …or perhaps even a lifetime.
        May we be instant and constant
           in awareness of the opportunity offered in each moment,
              …to bless, to redeem, or to restore,
              …for this too is part of the dream;
                 …and part of the greater dream yet,
                    …the Via de Cristo.   – Amen

Be My Valentine

As innocent as a first grade courtesy,
   ...as earnest as a timid declaration of first love,
      ...or as meaningful as the acknowledgment
      of decades of good marriage,
         ...hearts will be exchanged this week.

The inescapable heart imagery of valentines
   conveys the notion that something precious,
      – something of life itself –
      ...is offered for exchange with another
      for mutual safekeeping,
         ....perhaps for a lifetime.

As followers of Christ,
   we may use this moment in an even broader sense,
      ...to remind us that the preciousness and potential of *all*
      lie within our collective and individual stewardships.

So let this be our living valentine to one another,
   ...and to all who sojourn among us, however briefly,
      ...that we will be a people of openness, compassion,
      and loving-kindness;
      ...who offer time and space to recover and heal,
         ...to regain one's bearings and recover;
      ...and a people who foster fulfillment, significance, and joy,
      ...even if it costs us something of ourselves.

   ...Let this be our valentine today,
      ...from Via de Cristo,
         ...and in the Via de Cristo.   – Amen

Resurrection Day (Easter)

It is the season of resurrection even in nature,
   ...of things waking from the slumber of winter,
     ...to a season of new life.

For those in Christendom who gather in communion
  and celebration this morning,
    souls take wing in the beauties of tradition:
      ...the quiet presence of the lilies,
      ...the music, the drama, the familiar message,
       ...all connections with the passionate roots of our faith.

But we celebrate as well the story within the story;
  for Scripture surely does its truest work when it takes root
    and comes to life in us and among us,
      ...bringing new life, ...resurrected life, ...transformed life.

Holy Presence,
  the message to us of the cross now empty,
    and of the tombstone rolled away, is surely an open invitation;
  ...an invitation into the way of a resurrected life,
    ...even a transformed life;
      ...and the leaving behind of the shroud
       of all expectations save for the shalom of this Jesus.

And so today we celebrate not only the joys and hopes
  that flow from our Easter traditions,
    ...but also the very capacity found within us for metamorphosis.

We celebrate resurrection with those among us
  reawakened to things of meaning once lost or dormant.

We celebrate transformation with those among us who have abandoned
  the wounds and failings of what once was,
    for new wings of freedom and shalom.

And we celebrate those of us even now in transition,
  ...finding we are no longer the creatures we once were,
    ....but not yet realizing the fullness of what we are becoming;
    ...for that is our Easter way as individuals,
     ...and our Easter way as a people,
      ...as we walk in the Via de Cristo,
       ...in the Way of Christ.   – Amen

Mother's Day

Though not all of us have experienced it in just this way,
  there is something quite special about growing up
    in this village we call the church,
      ...this fellowship of kindred souls, ...when it is at its best.

In the beginning,
  we are shaped in the shelter and nurture of our mother's womb.
    ...And when the time is right, we are introduced to a new sanctuary
      ...in her arms and watch-care.

In the days and months and years that follow,
  we begin to be entrusted in measure into the hands,
    ...and then into the care,
      ...and then the teaching and example
        of others with whom we share a faith journey.

It is an easy expression of extraordinary trust that happens in this place,
  the coming to life of pledges made to each other
    in our celebrations of baptism and membership,
      ...of receiving one another into each other's concern and care.

So then let this be our celebration of mothers:
  ...that we honor her for who she is,
    ...for her trust, and her gifts entrusted to us;
  ...that her concerns *remain* our concerns,
    ...even as we lay groundwork and make preparations
      for mothers ...and children, yet to come;
  ...that we absorb and extend her best,
    ...spreading it like a gentle, nurturing, patient, forgiving,
      living, and hope-infused mantle over all that we do;

  ...for this too is the way we have been taught in the way of Christ,
    ...this Via de Cristo. – Amen

Pentecost

What must it have been like among Jesus' followers in that upper room,
    on this day set aside to celebrate the first fruits of harvest?
Surely little thought of joy,
    ...feeling so keenly the loss of their teacher no longer among them;
       ...weighed down in new uncertainties.

But then comes the sound of a wind that is not a wind,
    ...and flames that do not consume
       as they rest on each of those present;
    ...an attention-riveting, wordless and timeless message
       ...evidently fully grasped; ...evidently life altering.

Holy Presence,
    as we revisit this familiar story today
       – along with brothers and sisters around the world –
          we feel a peculiar resonance with the unmistakable message
          spoken through this imagery.

In another time of year,
    we echo and affirm that this message of Jesus is for all, as we pass
       – in near silence – a flame from a single candle to light another,
          ...each one then lighting yet another, ...and another,
             ...until our gathering is luminous with tens, or hundreds,
             ...perhaps innumerable lights,
               ...all individual flames, ...yet as one light,
             ...until all present are illuminated,
               without hesitation or precondition.

May this message carried into that upper room endure through us,
    ...remaining simple and timeless,
       ...a divine imprint that translates still
          into life-transforming freedom, and insight, and healing;
          ... still today piercing the barriers
          of custom and language.

And when our own moments of great opportunity and consequence come
    – even if not accompanied by a wind that is no wind,
       and flames that do not consume –
          may our voices be quieted,
            ...our attention rapt,
              ...lest we miss a transformational moment,
               here in the Via de Cristo. – Amen

Pentecost (Celebrate the Church)

Today, we celebrate Pentecost,
joining others around the world in revisiting the narrative of Scripture
that contains the roots of so many of our traditions,
...including the church as we know it.

Glorious painted images of the disciples,
and the visitation by the Holy Spirit of God,
reflect our age-old thinking about the beginnings of the church,
...about its workings, and its leaders.

But could it be that we perhaps missed something important
of what happened in that dimly lit room;
...and how transformation came to this huddled group
of disoriented and frightened disciples and friends?

Gracious God,
for all its flaws, still we celebrate church, ...though not its flaws.

We celebrate those who have walked with Jesus out of curiosity and hope,
...seeking your presence in his company.

We celebrate those who have spoken to us through the ages
of Jesus' message, and the understandings of those who followed him.

We celebrate those good hearts who created our traditions,
...and those who challenged them, ...who helped reshape them.

And so we also celebrate the church evolving,
...the movement that takes notice that we have not yet become
"thy kingdom come ...on earth";
...that takes notice that in Jesus, there is neither Jew nor Greek,
...neither slave nor free,
...neither male nor female,
...neither gay nor straight.

So may our celebrations lead to yet more faithful expression
of the ways of the one whose name we have taken.

May we recognize more fully that the church of Pentecost is us;
...yet perhaps less a church,
...and more a way,
...the way we call the Via de Cristo.   – Amen

Father's Day

To the one who needs no name we say, "Our Father."
To the one who needs no title we sing, "Our Father."

We pray, offering these words as high honor,
...addressing one transcendent,
...whom we picture as awesome in presence,
...powerful and just, ...perfect and constant in love.

Yet in our world, fathers fall short of that perfection.
Every father, ...every grandfather, ...every forefather,
...even the patriarchs of our faith,
...fall short.

And yet, ...reassuringly, ...and even profoundly,
...this Creation – all of it – has been declared "good,"
...even "very good."

And so, on this celebratory day, we are especially mindful of fathers;
...of fathers who have labored to balance
the demands of work, marriage, and children,
...at the pivot point between joy and sacrifice,
...of fathers lacking a good model, yet striving to be good fathers,
...of fathers who have not always been present for their children,
but labor now in love and support for grown children,
...of fathers wounded by the neglect and hostility of their children,
...of fathers with whom reconciliation remains elusive,
...of fathers who, though divorced,
have remained in their children's lives,
...of fathers of children adopted,
...of stepfathers, choosing the obligations and privileges of fatherhood.

And today, we are mindful as well of fathers
who hold a child yet in their heart, though lost to life,
...of men who have no children, but cherish others as if their own,
...of men who have fathered us as encouragers, mentors, and guides.

...and mindful of men about to become fathers,
anticipating the blessing of children.
...On this day, we are particularly mindful as well
of those whose fathers live now only in memory.   – Amen

Breathing Free (July 4)

Even as we gather together here this morning,
  we are a people, and a place of extraordinary privilege and opportunity.
The tradition of our nation invites,
  "Give me your tired, your poor, your huddled masses
    yearning to breathe free...,"[13]
And we of the Via de Cristo hear its echo, "Come to me,
  all who labor and are heavy laden, and I will give you rest."[14]

Gracious God,
  this morning, our thoughts turn to those who undertake the work
    of leveling the playing fields of law and culture,
      ...who choose to devote themselves to such risky
        and often dangerous work.

We acknowledge as well those who – in ways both large and small –
  give so freely of themselves and their substance
    in the creation of safety nets for those
      who have lost their handholds on wellness and security.

We lift up those who undertake the redemptive work of helping people
  lift themselves out of homelessness, and hope-crushing oppression.

We are grateful as well for those given the special abilities
  of bringing kindness and comfort
    into the world of those who have no such escape.

As we seek our own places in this work,
  may our hands not be found idle,
    nor our eyes blind to the injustices we encounter,
  ...finding instead our own ways to blunt the sharp edges
    of principle and contention,
  ...helping others understand that loaded words like
    "entitlement" and "welfare" mask real and desperate need,
      ...and that "amnesty" is just another word
        for forgiveness and redemption.

We – gathered here – are people of these promises,
  ...and trustees of this nation, and its ways.

And we are people of the Via de Cristo,
  ...remembering that we are the eyes and the hands of this Jesus
    who calls us to offer rest, ...and renewal, ...and forgiveness,
      ...seekers of peace, and space for breathing free.   – Amen

Belong (World Communion Day)

"Belong" is such a meaningful word:
    "You and I belong together!"
        Or perhaps, "I belong here!"

Whether chosen or discovered,
    such a moment speaks of a change in relationship,
        a sense of rightness,
            and a fullness of time and place and circumstance.

Who then are our brothers and sisters?
    ...All who choose to join us in worship, fellowship, or service,
        whether for an hour, a season, or a lifetime.

Who are our brothers and sisters?
    ...We who share communion worldwide,
        choosing to walk in the way of Christ.

And what binds us together?
    ...The presence and expression of Christ's perfect love.

Whether members or guests,
    whether friends alongside us or strangers in distant places,
        ...in this moment, we are all fellow pilgrims in your Creation,
            sharing the life that is your gift to us.

We belong to you, as does all of Creation,
    ...and in this moment,
        we celebrate belonging to each other as well.   – Amen.

Brothers & Sisters (World Communion)

Gracious God,
> today we are particularly mindful that we live in the providence
> > of one who is the God of all nations and peoples,
> > > whose creative impulse and expectations surely know nothing
> > > of the man-definitions and boundaries we create.

So who then are our brothers and sisters?

> We who stand together in this place, sharing in communion.

Who else are our brothers and sisters?

> We who share communion worldwide,
> > who walk alongside one another in the way of Christ.

Who else are our brothers and sisters?

Gracious God,
> we hear your call to draw the circle wider yet,
> > to neighbors and distant strangers alike
> > > who live with us elsewhere
> > > > in the beauty and benevolence of your Creation.

> But this is a harder thing for us,
> > and we don't yet know the exact way.

> But we do know that it is the right direction,
> > for your love, and your mercy
> > > surely extend to the ends of the earth.   – Amen

Cloud of Witnesses (All Saints Day)

Today, our thoughts are drawn to those who have passed from our midst,
  …lives that were – for a time too brief – intertwined with our own.

Leaving behind the unique imprint of their voices and their presence,
    they join a vast cloud of other witnesses
      who throughout time have shaped a spiritual legacy for us,
        …a legacy of understandings and practices
          that formed the foundations of our own faith journeys.

Gracious God,
    these saints we honor today,
      …whether beloved family to us or not,
      …whether encountered by intent or accident,
      …whether voices from the present or distant past,
    …are as surely a gift of your loving providence
      as the air we breathe, or the earth that sustains us.

So may we honor these saints, not only in *this* moment,
    but as we continue to handle with care their legacy to us,
      – this living message of providence and love and compassion –
        to be shared with all whose lives we touch;
          …and to be shared as well
            with those who will in time carry it forward
              to yet one more generation.

May this living message be so for these to come,
    even as it is for us.   – Amen

Thanksgiving

As we gather here this morning,
    away from the urgency and noise of the day-to-day,
      and of the approaching holidays,
      ...we pause to acknowledge the bounty that surrounds and sustains us,
        ...and to take notice of those blessings in particular
          that have brought us – sojourner and traveler alike –
            into this fellowship of kindred souls,
            ...into this place of worship,
            ...into this very moment in our varied faith walks.

Holy presence,
    how grateful we are
      for those who laid the foundations of our spiritual lives,
      ...who nurtured our sense of the Divine,
        and shaped our faith in earlier years;
      ...for those teachers, mentors, and others
        who patiently encouraged us in a growing faith;
      ...for those who drew us into fellowship and conversation,
        ...and into commitment and service;
      ...for friends who walked with us, and argued with us,
        and relentlessly loved us through loss
          and uncertainty and despair;
      ...for those who even now walk alongside us
        as we engage the doubts and questions
          and turning points of an evolving faith,

How grateful we are
    for that grand parade of God-seekers and believers who preceded us,
      ...who thought deeply, wrote timelessly,
        lived and taught courageously,
        ...and loved at great cost.

How in awe we are
    that you have entrusted into our inexperienced human hands
      this fruitful world, ...and its peoples, ...and its legacies.

May we grow gratefully and gracefully into their promise,
    ...and into your hope of what can be
      in the tomorrows yet to come.   – Amen

Dancing with God (Advent)

Fresh in our minds on this first day of Advent is the familiar story
  of the hope of all mankind being met in the birth of the Messiah.

But surely the gift of the Messiah is also a reflection of the Giver's hopes,
  …the hopes manifest in Creation,
    …the hopes now expressed as well in living human form.

The prophet Micah speaks of divine hope in his counsel
  to walk humbly with God, …to walk, …and listen
    …to take our time,
      …and notice,
        …to be with each other.

Another voice in our own time says further,
  "*The way we move through life, the way we interact with the world,
  the way we approach our place in the universe
  is the way that we dance with God.*"[15]

So may we walk humbly.
  …Perhaps better yet, …dance;
    …noticing, …feeling life's movements,
      …listening to its music, …tasting its sweetness,
        …experiencing a growing awareness of the divine work
          being born both in us, and among us.

As we enter this celebration of Advent, may we dance in joy,
  …dance in awe and wonder,
  …and dance in constant anticipation of the sacred moments,
    …the still points in a world that continues its spinning
      – unnoticing – around us.

And may it be that, "*The way we move through life,
  the way we interact with the world,
    the way we approach our place in the universe
    is the way that we dance with God.*"   – Amen

Hope (Advent)

- Today we light the Candle of Hope.

We are creatures of hope.
>   …Even as the light of a single candle drives away the darkness,
>>   it is hope that lights the way in the darkest places of life,
>>>   …and hope that draws us toward our better tomorrows.

Hope moves us deeply, and something within us dies without it.

But in the Via de Cristo, is hope about waiting patiently and anticipating?
Or is it about somehow becoming bringers of hope?

Gracious God,
>   we have just prayed, "your kingdom come, on earth as it is in heaven,"
>>   …and we understand this Advent hope to be about taking on
>>>   the work of fostering true peace and justice and righteousness
>>>   in the world you have given us.

May we keep hope alive to carry us,
    and our brothers and sisters
        over the dark segments of life.

May our work bring fresh hope to those worn down
    by circumstance and oppression.

May our examples nurture hope and generosity in our young.

May the light of hope shine through us wherever we are,
    …wherever we go,
        …and may your kingdom come, thereby, …on Earth.   – Amen

Love (Advent)

Christmas draws nearer still, almost here,
in celebration of the birth of the Christ Child
and all it represents for us.

Jesus' world was not unlike our own,
a rapidly changing world of discovery and power and exploitation,
...of walls and wars,
...of religion that has lost something of its luster,
and misplaced something of its soul.

Still, in some particularly undistinguished corner of this world,
we revisit the nativity as beautiful, ...as full of promise,
...a quiet, divine declaration of what is meaningful,
...and what is not,
...of the quiet workings of exquisite love,
...and of hope for what might yet be among mankind.

In these, our own moments,
even as we anticipate the celebration of this gift given us,
we turn our thoughts to what gifts we ourselves might bring
to honor this Christ of Christmas.

May our reflections of this love no longer be about our own feelings,
but the well-being of *all* the beloved of God;
...no longer about receiving,
but bearing life-altering redemption in all its forms to others,
even if it costs something of our selves,
...even if it costs something of our traditions.

In this time when all about us there is a building of walls,
may we bring gifts that speak of a love
that knows no boundaries,
a love blind to position and power,
...and heedless of the constraints of convention,
...bringing gifts that speak only of the unconditional love
we have come to know in the Via de Cristo,
...in the way of this Christ of Christmas.   – Amen

Peace (Advent)

The Peace Candle is once more alight in its Advent wreath;
   a flame that anticipates the celebration of the birth
      of the one called Jesus;
         …a flame that invites us to reflect on our deep need for peace,
         and our calling to be peacemakers.

We have often thought of this Jesus
   as the bringer of peace to a troubled world,
      …a peace at last universal and effortless.
And yet, our world remains in turmoil.

Divine Presence,
   we are realizing that peace is not a gift to be handed to us,
      …nor is it effortless.
Instead, it is a way to be walked,
      …a chosen way for us of the Via de Cristo,
      …and a way that calls us to action.

For where there are desperate people,
   there can be no peace.

Where there are marginalized who struggle
   for a place of dignity in our world,
     there can be no peace.

Where there is oppression of the most vulnerable,
   there can be no peace.

So let our work be among the desperate, the marginalized;
   among the oppressed, and the vulnerable.

May we practice peace, teach peace, and be peacemakers
   …wherever we are, …wherever we go.

"Let there be peace on Earth, and let it begin in me."[16]   – Amen

Trust (Advent)

In this Christmas season, how mindful we are of the star-strewn heavens,
   and their connection with the story of the one born Jesus of Nazareth.

We can't help but see these heavens a little differently in our own time.
   They humble us and make us feel very small.

Still, they also help us better understand ourselves,
    ...a curious combination of both creation and creator,
      ...and entrusted with the lives and well-being of ourselves
      ...and of our futures as never before.

Divine Presence,
   during this season, and all that it brings
     may we walk in awareness that the Via de Cristo is not so much
      about what has been given us,
        as what has been entrusted to us,
          ...to be, ...and to do, ...and use for good.

In our world, trust is built slowly, and broken easily,
   ...by persons, and by institutions.

So let us be a people, ...and a place, ...where trust is built,
   ...and trust is restored through faith walks
     that truly and faithfully bring light to dispel the darkness.

May our world, our children, and our futures
   be blessed through our trustworthiness,
     practiced here in the Via de Cristo.   – Amen

Courage *(Advent)*

This morning, on this third day of Advent,
    we have lighted a candle of courage.

Matthew's story of Mary and Joseph is a simple story,
    ...a very human story, ...and one of remarkable courage.

Often told as a story of uncertainty and obedience,
    ...there is surely also a lesser told story of passion and conflict,
        ...of respect and accommodation,
          ...and of love and commitment.

And courage must certainly have lighted their way
    as they reset the course of their lives to honor one another,
      and the God they served,
        ...even though it placed them at substantial odds
          with the social and religious expectations of the day.

Holy Presence,
    we continue to think
      – particularly during this season –
        about what has been given and entrusted to us
         through the life and teachings
           of the one born Jesus of Nazareth.

May we ponder as well what adjustments
    – or even new directions in our lives –
      would better reflect our discipleship.

And even as *we* begin redirecting *our* steps in that way
    – whether great or small in stride –
      may we feel this same courage as *our own* constant companion,
        as we absorb that courage too
          is a part of this Via de Cristo. – Amen

Mary's Gift

As Christmas draws closer yet,
    our attention turns toward Mary, the mother of Jesus,
        ...and to Scripture's prelude to the birth of the Christ Child.

How fortunate we are that early followers of the Christ
    preserved for us this disarmingly simple story
        of divine encounter and human response;
            and of the extraordinary courage
                summoned by an otherwise very ordinary teenager;
        ...of a girl of humble means
            about to be caught up in a most human of situations,
                ...yet the prologue to this most remarkable
                    Christmas story of divine love, and redemption.

Perhaps in Mary's story, we can find echoes of our own life,
    and even a part of her way that can become ours as well.

True Spirit of Christmas,
    may we, like Mary, take to heart the messenger's words to, "Fear not!"
        ...words of reassurance found throughout our sacred texts.

May we, like Mary, freely ask, "How shall this be?"
    giving voice with integrity to our own human uncertainties and doubts.

May we not be deterred in our work even when our answers
    – like Mary's –
        remain unresolved in mists of questions and wonder.

And may we find in Mary's accepting words
    our guidance when we too must summon courage for the work ahead,
        ...hearing Mary say not, "I will be the handmaid of the Lord,"
            ...rather, "I *am* the handmaid of the Lord,"
                ...for that is the key to courage in the Via de Cristo.   – Amen

Gratitude (Our Christmas Gift)

This morning, we look to the story of the Magi.
As these men of wisdom bring gifts to the newborn king of the Jews,
  we search the story for its message to us in our own day.

Though the gifts of the Magi were precious among men,
    and laden with significance,
      they seemed curiously of little real value to either this Jesus
        as an infant, or to the adult he was to become.

So what gifts might we ourselves, in our own time,
    choose on such an occasion as this,
      honoring the gift to us of this Christ Child?
Surely the Giver lacks nothing of the substance of this world.

Our hearts lead us to thoughts of offering love,
    …the finest thing of human experience we know.
      Yet in our heart of hearts, we surely know not how to love
        this One-Who-Was-Before-Everything-That-Is.

Perhaps then gratitude, a gift we are better able to understand;
    …yet not a gift to be given and left behind,
      …but the lighting of a steady flame of gratitude
        that each and every day stirs the creativity
          and sense of purpose that calls us.

May it be that just such a steady flame of gratitude
    lights our ways into this year before us, as yet unwritten,
      …illuminating ways that invite and bless, comfort and heal,
      …that redeem lives from the ravages of man and nature,
        …that in our unique ways extend compassion and loving-kindness
          beyond the reach of every other part of earth-Creation.

Let that, then, be our gift, …in the Via de Cristo.   – Amen

Light

In this season now upon us,
   trees are everywhere adorned with profusions of twinkling lights,
      inviting us once again into the timeless story of divine promise,
         ...and of its fulfillment found in the patterns of the stars
            on a certain night not so very long ago.

Light – wonderful and beautiful and life-giving –
   remains a universal metaphor for virtually all that is good.
So mysterious this light
   – sometimes one thing, sometimes another, yet always both –
      still eludes our understanding.
Yet, the very weakest of lights,
   benevolent in its energies, selfless in its giving,
      ...holds the power to banish an uncomprehending darkness.

Holy Presence, Source of All Light,
   we are reminded this morning of *our* call to be light in our world,
      for there are darknesses among our kind,
         ...confronted as we are every day
            by the shattered evidences of the worst that man can do.

May our choices and our movements
   bring new encouragement to the discouraged,
      hope to the despairing, peace to the troubled,
         healing to the hurting,
            and redemption to those who have lost their way,
   ...for we have ourselves been among these,
      ...when our own flames flickered and dimmed.

May that light – the light that is *you* made manifest in us –
   be shed abroad, ...even as it was through this Jesus,
      whose birth we celebrate with the lights of this season.
And in this new year approaching,
   may we find a new sense of privilege and adventure
      as we go about trimming our own special lights
         discovered in this Via de Cristo, the Way of Christ.   – Amen

Christmas Eve

Once again, in the quiet of this moment,
  we gather together as people of faith on Christmas Eve.

We are in the final hours of the final day in the Advent season,
  ...with the celebration of Christmas poised to greet us on the morrow.

Through our Advent observances, we have – in small measure –
  retraced the steps of those who long ago
    anticipated the coming of Messiah as foretold in Scripture.
And this is the night of promise.

Gracious God,
  may we feel afresh that sense of anticipation,
    yearning not for a gift wrapped in our own desires
      and expectations,
  but just as you prepared it and intended it,
    a disarmingly simple, living gift
      that over the ages continues to call us, ...and teach us,
        ...how to walk in awareness and gratitude
          before you in your Creation,
        ...and how to live in loving and just relationship
          with all those you have given us
            in a world of brothers and sisters;
        ...the walk we have come to call the way of Christ,
        ...the Via de Cristo.   – Amen

Christmas Continues

Our celebration of the birth of the Christ Child is now behind us.
   The carols are disappearing from the radio and the stores.
And we are preparing to take down the green,
      packing away the lights and ornaments,
         and sweeping away the last remaining evidences of Christmas.

But we create such occasions of celebration as remembrances,
   lest we forget things important to us.
Shall we so easily now pack away the passage of our year past,
   and simply resume our lives where we left off?

Or might we pause for a moment to reflect on its substance,
      and how its passage may alter our course into the New Year,
         …pausing a moment to reflect on which of our experiences to keep,
            and which to throw away,
         …to reflect on which of our mistakes and omissions
            to clothe in newfound awareness and intentionality,
               …and which to allow to fade in forgiveness?

May this be a time as well for revisiting our dreams of what might yet be,
      …for Christmas is, after all, about beginnings.

As we prepare to cross into this new year,
   let us raise a fresh evergreen vision of what might be.

   May its fragrances of compassion, kindness, humility,
         gentleness, and patience grace our lives.

   And may its ornaments be those of peace, …and hope, …and joy,
      …lighted with a thousand points of love.   – Amen

SPECIAL CIRCUMSTANCE

Call to Worship

In the Via de Cristo,
*we gather this morning in community
from many walks of life.*

We gather as one,
*united by the Spirit we have encountered;
united in serving, however our ways may differ.*

We seek in common
*to act justly and love mercy;
and to live well in the presence of the Divine.*

And this is our invitation,
*...this is our welcome to all who would journey with us,
learning to walk humbly with God,
in the way we call the Via de Cristo*

Communion Prayer

In these closing moments of our time together,
   we say to all here that this table,
      set in remembrance of Jesus, the Christ,
         remains open still.

May the presence of our host
   linger in our expressions of compassion and sacrifice,
      ...in our every offering of welcome and forgiveness.

And in our awareness and conversations,
   may we daily be drawn deeper still
      into Jesus' teachings,
         and Jesus' ways,
           ...in this Via de Cristo.   – Amen

Raising Children in the Faith

It is an extraordinary thing, this community of faith,
  …this gathering together of individuals and families
    in kinship of mind and spirit.
It has so many ways of being, …and blessing,
  and we would so like our children to experience
    and come to know personally the best of it.

And we wish that best to become a part of them
  as a foundation and framework for the
    sprouting and growth of a faith walk of their own,
      …one that can accompany them as they grow
        into independence and adulthood.

Gracious God,
  we are thoughtful today about parents and the community of faith
    walking hand in hand to help our children be aware of
      the interleavings of the realms of faith and living.

We are thoughtful about the witness to our children
  of a people gathered in community in search of the presence
    and purpose of the One Who Gives Us Being;

…thoughtful about parents sharing in openness and integrity,
  …through their living,
    …and in the power of our own words,
      …and our explanations of why we come together in this way;
        …why we follow the way of this Jesus.

May we live in constant awareness that we,
  …as parents, and as extended family, …and as no others,
    …convey to our children the authenticity of a lifelong faith,
      through the way our lives are expressed before them,
        …and to them.   – Amen

Baptism

This morning, we reflect on one of the milestones in Christian life.
Though differing in the specifics of understanding and practice,
   the sacrament of baptism is one of the ties that unify us
      in community with Christians around the world
         and throughout time.

Water – primal and life-giving –
   represents for us a spiritual transition, …leaving behind the old,
      …beginning anew in simplicity, grace, and loving-kindness.

Once again, a common thing – this ordinary water –
   has somehow been transformed into a messenger of the Divine.

Gracious God,
   may the very act of revisiting our own baptism this morning
      connect us afresh with the energy of that commitment
         to lifelong discipleship as learners and followers
            in the distinctive life-changing and life-fulfilling way
            shown us through the one called Jesus.

May our children learn from us
   that the essence of baptism is not simply a memorable waypoint,
      …but an intensely personal – and shared –
         acknowledgment of your presence and providence;
            an embracing of a grace-suffused life
               guided by and measured against
                  the teachings and example of this same Jesus.

And may this be witnessed by all
   as our collective voice of affirmation, and gratitude,
      …and as our invitation into the Via de Cristo.   – Amen

Continuity

It's a simple idea, and a time-honored idea,
  ...the Pastor as the shepherd
    – the one who knows all the places, and ways, and seasons –
    and the people as the flock,
      following his leading, and safe in his care.

But we have come to know that our relationship to the Divine
  is individual, truly coming to life only in one-to-one encounter,
    as we find our own unique balance among the questions,
      and circumstances, and the Mystery beyond them all.

And as the gathered people of Via de Cristo,
  ...as a fellowship of kindred minds and hearts,
    ...our way is much the same,
      ...finding our own collective and distinctive way
        of being the presence of the living God in a city,
          and in a world so much in need.

Gracious God,
  even as this is a time of transition, it is a time of new beginnings.

As individuals, we are but parts of what we are as a people,
  ...yet the substance from which our future will be shaped.

As a people, greater than the sum of those parts,
  we bring now together what we are, the synergy of community,
    and the blessings of legacy and our collective dream.

And with gratitude for those called to lead us,
  we embrace the mantle of continuity,
    ...as well as the uniqueness of gift and opportunity
      and collective vision that defines us,
        ...and with your blessing,
          continues to light the path before us.   – Amen

Comings and Goings

As our lives trace their individual ways through time and place,
    we find ourselves walking together here and there, ...for a time,
    ...and then moving on.

These confluences of our lives are no small matter,
    ...for as our lives flow as one for a time,
        we pass something of ourselves to one another,
           ...and we are changed,
              and the courses of our lives altered,
                ...perhaps a little, ...sometimes more.

But we are always somehow the better for having met.

May the best of our time together linger long with us all,
    ...lighting the way for works just begun in us.

Greg and Evelyn,
    our blessings go with you as you begin your new path.

May you be enriched by that part of us that travels with you,
    even as we are blessed by that part of you that continues in us.

Spirit of Grace,
    however these comings and goings mark our paths,
        we are privileged to remain one
           as brothers and sisters in "The Way,"
      ...continuing in our living and loving,
          learning and serving in the name of the Christ,
           ...and ever looking forward to
             – and seeking your direction for –
               whatever comes next. – Amen

Passages

Passages are everywhere in our lives, connecting one thing with another.
Yet, we're often quite unaware of them.
Still, day after day, they serve us as places of movement,
...of transition from where we were, ...to where we're going.

And once in a while, they are also pathways between who we were,
and who we are becoming.

Gracious God,
we are blessed by passages that connect our pasts and futures.
We need their space and time to ask questions,
to rethink important things,
and to make adjustments as slowly as they need to be made;
...as we leave behind portions of the old
and move toward the new.

We are blessed as well by the ever-present echoes in the hallways,
...the voices and lessons of the past,
the bearers of wisdom and patience,
and reminders of the passage into the present.

Though we are in most ways creatures of place, and of time,
we are grateful for always being works in progress,
...wonderfully designed to be in motion,
...questioning, exploring, learning, and adapting,
...and at times, lingering in the hallways to ponder.

Dear Giver of Life,
we are grateful for these passages between living spaces,
...and between our understandings.
Whether the path be straight or crooked, the destination clear or not,
we take strength from the constancy
and reassurance of your presence,
...and of your hope in us as we journey.   – Amen

Migration and Change

Here in the heat of summer, we long for the yellow leaves of fall,
    and the graceful vees of the migrating wildfowl
        as they follow the seasonal warmth southward.

It's these graceful creatures of the air
    that frame our thinking for today,
        so clear in their purpose,
            ...and their direction.

In their flights, they once again honor their seasonal call
    to extraordinary individual and community effort,
        ...toward a place of change that not only sustains them,
        but makes way for their young,
            and for generations yet to come.

May we borrow from their ways,
    as a season of change is upon us as well,
        ...finding clarity of purpose,
            for ourselves, and our fellowship;
        ...defining direction,
            for ourselves, and our fellowship;
        ...doing our parts, even as our roles change,
            ...leading and following,
                ...following and leading,
                    ...and helping one another when we fall behind.

May it be so.   – Amen

Heavy Lifting

Sooner or later, we are all touched by circumstances
    that shatter us with momentous change, or injury, or loss.

Mercifully, with the passage of time, the mists of numbness and shock
    begin to lift, …a little.
        Though wobbly, we struggle to our feet.
        Though dimly, we see vaguely a path ahead.

But for now, it is a way troubled still by the remaining voids,
    …and silences, …and unanswered questions.

It is the time of heavy lifting for us in our disarray and heartache.

In such a time, we are so in need of a sense of divine presence,
    …of the capacity you have created within us to recover and heal,
        …and perhaps a special one to accompany us on our way.

A measure of heavy lifting is ours as well when we are called to share
    the intimacy and vulnerabilities of one in such a time of recovery.

Gracious God,
    we are in need of wisdom to sense when
        and how we may have a place in the healing process
            of our grieving brothers and sisters.

Our prayer is to be able to hear well the voice of an overflowing heart,
    whether spoken or unspoken,
        …to be a comfort when possible,
            …to be an agent of grace when it isn't,
                …and to know always the light that marks the dawn
                of a new day somewhere just ahead.   – Amen

Hard Choices

From time to time, all of us find ourselves in difficult situations
  ...where neither minds that reason nor hearts that feel
    give us a clear view of what to do.

Though these hard places come without instructions,
  ...or sometimes with too many answers, all imperfect,
    ...nevertheless, we find we must choose,
      ...or we must act.

Gracious God, you are our light and our refuge.
  But you have made us in your special way,
    and you seem to have entrusted such moments to us.

When we alone must make a hard choice,
  help us to reach down to foundations
    we have built carefully in the quiet times.

And on those occasions when we must *act* quickly,
  though our confidence is not high,
    and our choices difficult and less than clear,
      may what we have absorbed of you in our minds,
        and hearts, and bones,
          guide us in such a moment.

Against just such a day,
  may "The Way" be absorbed as a living framework in our being,
    so that when we must choose, or act in the moment
      – however uncertainly or imperfectly –
        ...there remains always the refuge of your grace.   – Amen

Inbound Hope

We have been made so that, somehow, in our humanity,
  we cannot live long in the absence of hope.

And yet, in that same humanity, we can find ourselves suddenly
  in a life place where helplessness and darkness deepen
    as the candle of hope within us flickers and dims.

Gracious God,
  you are our wellspring of life, ...and of hope.

May we – in those darkest hours before dawn – learn to lean into you,
  ...and to begin to make room anew for the warmth and light
    that is the reassurance of your presence and being.

You have given us a community of brothers and sisters,
  who have covenanted to walk together with one another,
    in good times and bad.

May we – in these darkest of hours –
  be unashamed and unafraid to reach for a hand to steady us,
    ...or for a companion to help find our new way.

We know – as followers in "The Way" –
  that we are to learn to let love flow unhindered outward.
    But it may be a harder thing to invite love to flow freely inward,
      even when we are in greatest need.

May we learn to allow grace and hope and love flow freely
  ...in both directions.   – Amen

After the Mountaintop[*]

What would we do without the mountaintop experiences,
   those exhilarating highs, …the views,
      the sense of accomplishment and pure joy that we find there?

But the mountaintops are not places for living,
   …only blessed parentheses in life,
      …and then we must begin to work our way back down the slopes,
        …where life is no longer simple,
         where visibility is not as clear,
           …and time is once again a precious thing.

Holy Presence,
   may we truly absorb the Way of Jesus,
      not striving for elusive mountaintop experiences,
        but discovering afresh the fulfillment found
          in the realization of our full potential
            in the everyday walks within your Creation.

May we husband well our work in the valleys,
   …fostering justice and mercy,
      touching people and changing lives.

May we nurture as well the opportunities of the slopes,
   …putting to work imagination and creativity
      to overcome momentary obstacles, realize hopes,
      and build a better future.

And may we find ourselves instant and constant in gratitude
   …for the work ever before us,
      …and for The Way within us that lights our paths.   – Amen

Dreams Deferred

Dreams are among the most powerful experiences of humankind.
As they take shape at the intersection of imagination and possibility,
they are the prelude to every blessing and opportunity
that lies just ahead.

Dreams are an intimate calling, energizing us, activating our passions,
and drawing us into new and risky endeavors
that can bring into being that which has never been before.

But, we also find it terribly easy to put aside our dreams
in the face of uncertainty or priorities.
So what then shall we do with dreams deferred?

Creative Presence,
may we be constantly mindful that our dreams, too,
are part of our stewardship.

Though our dreams be deferred,
may we neither forget,
nor easily forfeit them for those of another.

May we be attentive when our dreams begin to ask,
"Is this now the time? ...Or the place?"

May we find the courage to step into the dream, as helper, or as leader,
when it speaks to our heart.

And may the dreams that we are privileged to enter into bring blessing,
whether in small ways or great,
whether in the present,
or in preparation for generations to come.   – Amen

Interceptions (Super Bowl)

What is it about that word, "interception"?
In a moment, it commands our attention;
...the game has changed, control has shifted,
plans and expectations have been knocked off course.

Gracious God,
we acknowledge that we
– both as individuals, and in community –
are still works in progress when it comes to responding
to interceptions that involve our faith journeys.

In such a moment in our lives,
...may we learn to respond by reaching for a next higher priority,
the next higher principle or vision,
as our guide for reestablishing our bearings.

And when we become restless in the sameness of receiving,
...may we learn to consider service,
...reaching toward the higher calling
of giving of what we are, and of what you are in us.

When slowed or detoured by conflict, or hurt,
or disappointment, or even dislike,
...may we reach toward the higher calling of love,
to restore and replenish our hearts,
and reenergize us for the greater work ahead.

And whenever and wherever we encounter injustice,
...may we see with your eyes, ...seeing possibilities everywhere,
...not just in others,
...but even in ourselves as we find ways to respond,
reaching toward the higher miracle of transformation,
...or perhaps redemption of a life adrift.   – Amen

Disaster

Gracious God,
today we are especially mindful that the security we know
can be so easily and suddenly shaken,
…or even lost.

The images of those caught up in devastation and loss are so painful
we want to turn away.
But in your patience, we are learning how not to do that.

Instead we are learning to turn our sense of church inside out;
…realizing that the real work of the church in the world
lies outside our sturdy and opaque walls.

And so we are learning to change the way we see;
…that the real work of the church begins
with turning our eyes, and our feet,
toward those who are in pain and need.

And we are learning the still harder lesson,
to turn our hearts inside out as well;
…to feel the pain and need as if it is our own
– as if it is *my* own –
and to respond with newfound compassion.

Gracious God,
we have come to know that your love moves on our two feet,
and reaches through our two hands,
…if only our eyes see,…and if our hearts direct.

In this moment,
it is our prayer to learn to be your living, breathing presence
…in every place where love and solace
and healing are in desperate need,
…whether it be at arm's length,
or half a world away.   – Amen

Moving Toward the Other (Post 9-11)

On this day of national remembrance,
  we turn our thoughts to the ways of Jesus
    as our guide through this difficult portion of our journey.

The Via de Cristo we have chosen is not a way of hate or fear.
  And yet, when loss and anger are real and near,
    we may struggle to stay the course of peace,
      reconciliation, forgiveness,
        ...and relationship with those we identify with our loss.

Divine Presence,
  ...in the way of Christ,
    may we be mindful that most within warring nations
      have little in common with those who engage in violence,
        but are victims instead, even as we have been.

We don't yet know how to heed your high calling to love even our enemies.
  Until then, may we draw on the civility and grace that we have learned.

In the way of Christ, may we oppose the injustices in our own nation
  born of the conflicts on distant shores.

May we, in the way of Christ, continue to seek individual ways
  to reach beyond the bounds of tradition and apprehension
    to be a blessing to all those we encounter,
      regardless of their differences from us.

May we choose not to detour around these Samarias of our lives,
  but to walk through them,
    ...even as Jesus did.   – Amen

Lord's Prayer

We know this prayer so well.
　　We know it by heart; we sing it; we speak it; we hear it with our hearts,
　　　　and it never fails to quiet our soul.

Though not always registering and savoring every word;
　　…still we speak it to one another in community,
　　　　a sacred mantra that draws us into your presence.

But we would know better the message etched so carefully
　　in these few words. So we ask, teach us too to pray.

"Our Father, in heaven…," it begins,
　　yet we have come to know you
　　　　as one who transcends earth-kind relationship,
　　　　　　who exists without where-ness;
　　　　　　　　…who needs no encumbrance of name.

　　So teach us more fully this new way of knowing you,
　　　　…an abiding presence,
　　　　　　even as our understanding and awe ever deepens.

"Give us this day …," it continues,
　　yet we sense that your desire and hope in and for us
　　　　is in some way bigger than the day.

　　Though your providence blesses us every moment of every day,
　　　　may we learn to reach beyond the bounds
　　　　　　of only the daily, and the personal.

"Thy will be done on Earth…"

　　No longer a monarchy, with its castle beyond the dome of the stars,
　　　　we sense that your kingdom has somehow become us;
　　　　　　…and we have a way yet to go.

So may we learn how to live in this new way of being,
　　…of being the unfailing presence of love among our own,
　　…of loving the least of these our brothers and sisters,
　　…of loving our neighbors even as ourselves,
　　　　…and learning to somehow even reach out in love
　　　　　　to those we have called enemies,
　　　　　　　　because the idea of "enemies" is surely alien to you.   – Amen

Twelve Steps

Today we celebrate and reflect on the extraordinary restorative success
    of a path with neither denomination,
        nor gathering place of its own.

Though different from our own in some of its ways,
    yet it seems familiar in others.

Alike, we experience the need for community,
    ...the sharing among ourselves of our experiences, lessons, and insights.

Alike, we experience together the value of mutual support,
    ...the sharing of ourselves in the presence of need.

Alike, we recognize the value of accountability,
    ...as we strive to measure unflinchingly our consistency
        in walking in the presence and providence of our Higher Power.

So in these moments,
    we celebrate in common the transcendent and creative presence
        that gifts us with healing and restoration and wholeness of life,
            whether by the Twelve Step path,
                or another which we have found,
                    ...or for some of us, ...both.   – Amen

Islamic Guests

This morning, we are from two great faith traditions,
 and yet we share much in common.
  Though we use different names,
   …even a hundred different names,
    to address the Creative One Who Needs No Name,
   …are they not just how we speak
    of one and the same Creative Impulse
     that brought into being all that is, or ever has been?

Though we differ in our ways,
 do not our roots grow in the same soil of Abraham's journey?

Do not the practices of our faith express one and the same thirst
 for encounter with the Divine?

Do we not hunger for a life suffused with awe and gratitude and humility?
 …for a journey traced in human kindness and creativity?

And do we not also share a common burden of some among our kind
 who tragically misunderstand and misrepresent
  the beauty and benevolence of the One who brought us into being?

Spirit among us, may we learn to set aside our man-differences,
 until what matters to us is transformed into what matters to you.

May we learn to glimpse in each other
 the image of sacred hope and promise etched into our beings.

May we learn from one another; …be enriched by one another;
 …no longer sundered by our differences,
  but growing and healing in community
   as we give greater honor and freedom to your presence
    within and among us.   – Amen

Buddhist Guests

In this special space this morning, we are two long traditions
    viewing each other through a most curious window.
We see some differences in appearances;
    …we know of differences in understandings and ways,
      …and we hear many differences in the words we use
        to name and describe the deep things of life.

And yet, though we hear and heed the voices of two different teachers,
    we seem to find certain similarities in our movements in life.

So, may it be in the days to come
    that we can grow in recognition of each other as more than travelers
      whose lives have somehow intersected,
    …perhaps discovering things familiar in one another,
      …as well as things different from which we may learn
        more of our place and way of being in this unfolding universe.

May it be that we can find new ways of signaling respect
    and encouragement to one another
      as we work toward the realization of the full potential
      of what we are, and what we can be,
        …as positive and healing presences in our world.

May we find new ways of working together
    to reduce and prevent suffering in the world,
    …and obstructing exploitation of kindred souls.

May we be thoughtfully vigilant against spending our lives frivolously,
    or trivially, or presumptuously.

May we instead be instant and constant
    in our pursuit and practice of wisdom, and virtue,
    …of empathy and compassion,
      …and of loving-kindness.   – Amen

ABOUT THE AUTHOR

I offer these writings as a lay person, actively involved in church life in one way or another, for the whole of my 70-some years. Most of those involvements lay in the areas of adult Bible study, music, and media. A master's degree in physics from Arizona State University enabled me to also enjoy a venturesome and rewarding career in technology development in the aerospace community.

Living and working in both of these worlds, I always had a sense that there ultimately existed a discoverable harmony where they intermingled, and a certain balance elsewhere. The resulting questions and musings, and the evolutions of my perspectives over the years, eventually led me from the benevolent, but conservative evangelical Christian church settings of my younger years, toward those of a Progressive Christian community. In time I found a better fit under the umbrella of the United Methodist Church.

It was there - in my sojourn with Via de Cristo United Methodist Fellowship - that I was began contributing regularly to the written liturgical content of the worship services, …much of which finds its way into this collection. It was a new adventure for me, and ultimately a remarkable source of stimulation and challenge in my own spiritual journey.

In the larger picture, My wife and I bask in the sense of privilege we experience as living, sentient souls in this unfathomable and benevolent Creation, in the glorious ambience of the American Southwest, and in the company of wonderful and interesting friends, which of course includes those found in the Via de Cristo community. We're proud of our two sons, and the work they have chosen, and watch as the promise of the next generation develops in the hands of our three bright and high-energy grandsons!

ENDNOTES

---

[1] Title and content inspired by a sermon of Dr. Tex Sample

[2] Wildly descriptive title of a blog authored by Jon Zuck, *The Wild Things of God*, http://frimmin.com

[3] "Thin place" – a Celtic description of a time or place where the veil between ourselves and the domain of the divine seems particularly "translucent"

[4] Alluding to a wonderful Isaac Newton brachistochrone legend whose punch line is a compliment paid Newton, "One recognizes the lion by his paw prints."

[5] Galatians 3:3

[6] Galatians 3:28

[7] From the United Methodist Baptismal Covenant

[8] John 15:13

[9] Micah 6:8b

[10] Matthew 5:5; Psalm 37:11

[11] From *Behold the Beauty of the Lord*, by Henri Nouwen

[12] Words of poet Annie Flint, as adapted into the hymn, *Grace Greater than Our Sin*

[13] From the sonnet, *"The New Colossus"* by Emma Lazarus, immortalized on a bronze plaque inside the Statue of Liberty

[14] Matthew 11:28

[15] Rev. J. Carl Gregg; http://broadviewchurch.net/2010/11/sermon-hail-mary-full-of-grace/

[16] Opening words from familiar song, *Let there be peace on Earth* by Vince Gill

[17] Title and content inspired by a sermon by Rev. Tom Kiracofe

48409406R00086

Made in the USA
Lexington, KY
29 December 2015